A cat on the Camino de Santiago

Pia Lamm

For my Mum, who teached me to roar...

INHALT

—

I want to visit a friend. More precisely, his grave. I haven't been there yet, even though he died quite a long time ago. We weren't particularly close, but we are quite similar. Unlike him, I am not from the Mediterranean region, but I am just as hot-tempered. I believe he could always empathize with me very well, especially when I clashed with a Franconian pastor. In his homeland, he was nicknamed „Son of Thunder." He is buried in Spain, so I will travel most of the way by plane, but then walk several hundred kilometers on foot.

Alright, let's call it what it is — I am going on a pilgrimage on the Way of St. James — Camino de Santiago. But the thing about the friend was absolutely serious. Saint James is my favorite apostle. Not only because he was apparently quite a choleric. He was also one of the three whom Jesus took to Mount Tabor, where He revealed Himself to them in His transfigured form, in His divine glory, with Moses and Elijah. Despite this incredible experience, James was not at the cross. Only his brother and Jesus' mother were there. And I am also a coward who sometimes backs out at the crucial moment. But in the end, James was the first apostle to die a martyr's death, and that gives me hope.

1. Navarrete

In 2018, my mother and I arrive in Logroño by train from Bilbao. We start our journey quite late in the full sun and heat. Initially, the path goes through the city itself, so we use the shade of the buildings as much as possible. We treat ourselves to an ice cream at a supermarket. On the outskirts of the city, the Camino passes through a large park with huge oleander bushes, slender cypress trees, and irrigation systems with little rainbows fanning out over the water sprays. We also discover interesting trees with long yellowish leaves like ribbons.

The path then leads directly by the reservoir – Pantano de la Grajera – in the scorching sun. Several bike pilgrims zoom past us, and I envy them. I wish I had a bike to quickly escape the sun. Luckily, soon after, we come across a stretch of forest with a few benches where we gratefully collapse. Squirrels play around us.

West of the reservoir, we come across a small wooden hut – Ermita del Peregrino Pasante. Marcelino is a Camino veteran. He has walked the way many times since the 70s. In the 80s, he even did it in medieval clothing he made himself. Now, he greets other pilgrims passing by his hermitage. We also get our pilgrim passports stamped and refill our water bottles. I keep hearing this – once you get a taste for walking the Camino, it never leaves you. It's true; this is my third time (my mother's second), and I hope it's not the last.

But what is pilgrimage actually? Interestingly, almost every religion in the world has its pilgrimage sites, customs, and rules. Two elements are found in all these pilgrimages – the destination, usually a saint's grave or an apparition site, and the journey, which in human history was mostly done on foot while practicing certain religious rituals along the way. Why do people say today, especially about the Camino, that the journey is the destination? Probably to emphasize the role of the journey. Nowadays, you can just hop on a plane to Santiago, Rome, or Jerusalem. It's very practical and convenient, but you risk forgetting that you need to prepare for visiting a holy place. The journey itself is indeed an important reason for making the trip. However, if we lose sight of the destination, the journey loses its meaning.

What makes pilgrimage so universal is that it is actually a metaphor for life. In life, it's about two things: the goal we want to reach in the end and how we travel the path. Unfortunately, for many today, the journey has indeed become the goal. And then the (life) pilgrimage becomes just a simple hike. It can be beautiful and good for you, but it can quickly happen that you are actually just going in circles, around yourself. And let's be honest, if there is no goal, why should one behave decently along the way? If the journey is everything, then having fun is the only thing that matters.

The path now leads up and down through green hills often covered with vineyards, then a long stretch along the main

road, practically without any shade. On the median strip, oleanders bloom beautifully again, alternating white and pink. Since
my penultimate visit to Rome, I have been a huge fan of these
bushes. I even have one at home that I grew from a seed, and
it has been blooming white for three years now – the only plant
besides aloe that tolerates me.

On the left hill, a silhouette of a bull points in the other
direction, probably towards Pamplona. Finally, Navarrete appears before us. We are now walking on a gravel-sand path
between the vineyards. The mix of sun, heat, and dust is really
taking a toll on us. The wine ads along the way make us even
more aware of our thirst. The sign „Hospital de Peregrinos San
Juan de Acre" only refers to the 30 cm high ruin we pass by.
So, we have to keep going.

Upon arriving at the hostel, we treat ourselves to a cold lemonade and a few hours of sleep, and in the evening, we go back
to the center for the evening Mass. At the end of the service,
I hear for the first time the Spanish original of Pope John Paul
II's favorite song:

„Señor, me has mirado a los ojos sonriendo has dicho mi
nombre en las arena he dejado mi barca junto a ti buscar otro
mar" – „O Lord, You have looked into my eyes / smiling,
You have spoken my name / On the sand, I have left my
boat / with You, Jesus, I begin my catch."

Am I on the path Jesus has called me to? Am I following Him, or am I just going in circles around myself? I have to ask myself this question repeatedly and adjust my course if necessary. In the church stands a figure of Saint Roch. By now, I no longer confuse him with James – Roch usually has a dog with him and wounds on his knees. But why? I need to research that further.

Now, we first indulge in the famous garlic soup, still bubbling on the table, and some good red wine – after all, we are still in La Rioja.

2.   Najera

Now that was an achievement – we're on the road before sunrise, already fueled by coffee. Walking at sunrise always reminds me of the pilgrimages to our national Marian sanctuary. There's a special song that comes to mind every time I see the rising sun. Unfortunately, I can only remember fragments of the lyrics, so I pull out my phone and promptly find the right recording online. My mother also loves the little Marian breviary, long forgotten in Germany, with its full title: „*Little Office oft he Immaculate Conception.*" I remember as a child, the women in our village church always sang it before the early Mass and then on the foot pilgrimages at sunrise as the first song and prayer.

„*Come, my lips, now announce the praises and proclamations of the blessed Virgin".*

However, the title always makes me smile. I remember all the conversations, TV reports, and articles where the Immaculate Conception is confused with the virginal conception. It's actually simple – just look at the calendar and it all becomes clear. In March, nine months before Christmas, we celebrate the Annunciation, the day when Jesus was virginally conceived in Mary's womb by the Holy Spirit. The Feast of the Immaculate Conception, however, is celebrated on December 8th, exactly nine months before September 8th – Mary's birth. This is when we remember that Mary was conceived by her mother Anna, immaculately, meaning without the stain of original sin. Unlike all of us, who come into the world with original sin and only receive sanctifying grace through baptism, Mary was free from it from the beginning. The angel said to her, *„Hail, full of grace!" (Luke 1:28)*. She was full of grace, free from any sin, both personal and original.

„From eternity the Lord has preordained you,
Mother of the only-begotten Word, by whom He created
Earth, sea, and sky: He adorned you beautifully
as His Bride, who did not sin in Adam".

The morning freshness feels really good. Vineyards upon vineyards bordered by small hills – a true feast for the eyes. It feels like we're in Austria. The Weinviertel Jakobsweg five years ago looked quite similar. The sun peeks between the clouds, and walking in this beautiful green environment is a pleasure. Apart from one tractor, we haven't encountered anyone so far. Suddenly, we notice footprints in the sand ahead of us – not from shoes, but bare feet. Someone is walking the Camino barefoot. Could it be a special form of penance?

There are no places to stop for a break today. So we add 600 meters and take a little detour to Ventosa halfway through. There, we discover the barefoot pilgrim. With his guitar and long colorful clothes, he looks more like a hippie than a penance-oriented Catholic. His hiking boots are dangling from his backpack, so maybe he just wanted to feel the warm sand underfoot. On the terrace of the „Buen Camino" bar, we leisurely drink coffee, eat tortilla and muffins, and call home.

My husband is probably still sleeping, but we definitely call Dad. He's a bit worried that my mother, at 70 years old, is undertaking such a hike, so we check in with him every day.

We continue on. Nine kilometers still lie ahead of us. It's getting really warm, and I feel a sore spot on my thigh. Cotton underwear is not automatically the best for long hikes.

The path continues on field tracks between vineyards and fields, then along the main road, past some industrial buildings and construction sites. Just before Nájera, there's a small park, and the sight of the benches is very tempting. However, we remain steadfast, fearing the prospect of walking in even greater heat.

The path leads between gardens, and at one property, there is a water tap, a table, and two benches under a roof. Several Camino poems and, of course, pilgrim advertisements are posted here. We pour the lukewarm water from our bottles over ourselves, wet our hats, pant legs, and shirts – in this sun, I prudently wear long sleeves – and refill our bottles with the cold water provided by a friendly garden owner..

In the city, the heat is even worse, and our hostel is again at the end of the town. So we dive into the first open bar, enjoying a cold cider and a large ham baguette. The bar's air conditioning makes it hard to leave. But the bed is only 900 meters away. We first have to cross the bridge over the Najerilla River into the old town.

This part of Nájera seems to cling to the steep red-brown rock wall, and the sight makes me uneasy. Luckily, our hostel isn't too close, but the Monasterio de Santa Maria la Real a few hundred meters away seems to be partly built into the wall. The narrow streets here are decorated with colorful medieval-looking flags. Apparently, there's a festival around this time.

Once in the room, I first upload some photos to my blog, then we sleep. The rhythm on the Camino more or less matches the rhythm of the people living here. You try to finish your day's hike before the siesta and then collapse, exhausted, into bed during the hottest part of the day. After a good nap, you can then take care of food or sightseeing once the shops and restaurants reopen after 5 pm.

Today is Sunday, and according to the information on the internet, there should be a Holy Mass in the evening at the Church of the Cross. Unfortunately, we find the church closed. Thankfully, we managed to attend the evening Mass yesterday.

For today, there's only one thing left on the agenda – dinner. But in this heat, we don't have much of an appetite. So we share a portion of turkey breast with salad and fries and stock up on our water supplies.

3.   Cirueña

The first stretch today is quite steep. We have to climb the hill that we saw directly behind the old town yesterday. There are plenty of pilgrims on the road, and among them, some tractors. The path cuts into the hill, with pine-covered slopes on both sides. Just when we think we've almost reached the highest point, it turns out the path only makes a loop here. We know this effect well from the Wachau. There, too, we often believed that it couldn't go any higher because we could only see the sky. Yet, it usually turned out that there was still further to climb. By now, my mother no longer believes me when I say the ascent will soon end.

Eventually, of course, it does end, and at the top, there are no more pines, just red soil and vineyards. Slowly, it becomes flat and green. Along the path run concrete channels, which apparently irrigate the vines. On the horizon, we can see a mountain panorama in the light mist. In Azofra, we take a beer and coffee break at a bar aptly named ‚El Descanso del Peregrino'. The photo-framed map on the wall shows all the Caminos the owner has walked himself, with the years marked. Maybe we'll make something like that for our home someday.

We've now left the vineyards behind. The path leads through fields of grain. Some have already been harvested. Instead of green, the area now shines wheat-yellow. Our hostel in Cirueña is also next to a grain field, separated only by a path, at the edge of the village. I take our laundry to the washing machine in the basement and pause at this scene. The combination of warm yellow and sky blue has always delighted me. Perhaps the sight is so calming because we unconsciously associate the view of ripe grain in good weather with a good harvest and thus security? Maybe that's why so many businessmen wear these colors? The modern albergue, apparently built recently, contains quite a bit of antique furniture and decor. A beautiful old statue of Christ the King on the throne greets pilgrims right at the entrance. Other items here also seem to have been saved from one or several churches during a post-conciliar cleanup.

Tonight, there's a communal dinner. I really enjoy these gatherings at the big table with many other pilgrims and manage to persuade my mother to join by promising to act as a translator. The group tonight is quite Romanesque-speaking. A few older Spaniards and an Italian couple with a son who, fortunately, speaks some English. This way, there's not much for me to translate. One group speaks Spanish, the other responds in Italian. After an introductory round, which we managed with a little English help, I have no choice but to try to understand some fragments of the further conversation.

„Do you believe in God?" the young man suddenly asks me in English, having apparently noticed our sign of the cross before the meal.

„Yes," I smile.

He leaves it at that and turns back to the other participants. It still amazes me that people on the Camino de Santiago are surprised that someone believes in God. Isn't it kind of strange? You walk one of the most famous Christian pilgrimage routes and are surprised to meet Christians. My colleagues in the IT and business sectors are even more astonished when I pray before lunch, but there it surprises me less.

When I think about it, I have never really doubted God's existence. I can't recall a specific event where I particularly felt His presence, but the fact that He exists was always logical and therefore certain to me. The arguments of Thomas Aquinas, which we learned in school – that there must be a first cause because everything we observe has a cause – were convincing enough for me. But when I consider the complexity of the human brain, or the whole body, let alone the entire world, God's existence is practically proven to me. There can be no more plausible explanation. You might as well expect a gust of wind to blow the grains of sand on the beach into the model of Cologne Cathedral. Probability theory rules that out. And the creation of our world without a creator is even more incredibly unlikely. Besides, I can't imagine that the intuition of countless billions of people all over the earth and throughout time – that there is a higher power – could simply be wrong. Even according to the theory of evolution, this development seems illogical unless it reflects a fact. Especially when you consider that people often go against their survival instincts because of this belief.

So I ponder while gathering our laundry in the evening. It has indeed dried within a few hours.

4.   Santo Domingo de la Calzada

Today there is no blue sky. A thick, uniform layer of clouds hangs above us. As long as no rain falls, it's fine. It's almost a pity that we only plan to walk 7 kilometers today.

At the roundabout, there's a pilgrim silhouette and a large stylized metal scallop shell. Shortly after, the Camino turns off the asphalt onto a dirt road. The path remains very pleasant, running between grain fields over gentle hills. Several cycling pilgrims whiz past us. Under the gray sky today, the fields don't look bright gold but slightly orange. The mountains on the horizon are barely visible in the mist, and it actually drizzles a bit now and then. The first four and a half kilometers pass quickly. The rest of today's path leads through the outskirts of Santo Domingo de la Calzada. The town and cathedral are named after Saint Dominic of Silos (not to be confused with the founder of the Dominican Order, who came from near

Burgos but lived about 100 years later and was active not only in Spain but also in France and Rome). This Dominic lived in the area as a hermit and a great supporter of the pilgrims to Santiago. He built a bridge over the Oja River and a pilgrim hospital, renewed roads, and dedicated his entire life to pilgrims. Now he has a beautiful tomb in the Gothic cathedral that bears his name. There is also a rather bizarre attraction in the cathedral: a chicken coop, located opposite Dominic's tomb in the south transept. According to legend, a young pilgrim was accused of theft by an innkeeper's daughter, whose advances he had rejected. After a short trial, he was hanged, and his parents continued to Santiago. On their return journey, however, they found their son alive. He said that Saint Dominic had held him up. When the judge heard this, he said the man was as dead as the roasted chickens on his plate. At that moment, the chickens stood up and fluttered away. The pilgrim was released, and the deceitful innkeeper's daughter was punished.

From here, we take the bus to Burgos. This time, we're doing the Camino piece by piece, comfortably and like a vacation, so to speak. My mother says that I'll have to do the next hikes without her. But in 30 years – when she is 100 – she'll definitely come along again. By then, I will be 70 myself. Yes, I'm taking her at her word; the date is set.

Along the way, I recall the chicken miracle and an even greater miracle that proves not only the existence of God but also
the truth of Christianity – the resurrection of Jesus. Throughout history, there have been some magicians and miracle
workers, and even the Old Testament attests that Pharaoh's
magicians could replicate some of Moses' miracles. But there
is no one other than Jesus Christ who proved his mission by
conquering death. First, he raised his dead friend Lazarus, who
wasn't roasted like the chickens but had already been dead for
a few days and stank, and then he himself rose on the third day
after his crucifixion and burial. Josh McDowell analyzes the
resurrection testimonies according to modern judicial rules in
his book and finds them absolutely credible. What convinces
me even more, however, is the fact that almost all witnesses to
this event died as martyrs for this truth – and so did many of
their followers. At least for me, it is inconceivable that someone would allow themselves to be tortured and killed for a lie.
And why am I convinced by the Catholic Church? Because
after thorough analysis, I clearly see that it continues to teach
exactly what we can read in the oldest writings of the apostles
and church fathers from the first centuries. Also, because this
teaching is absolutely logical, consistent, and coherent.

5.   Burgos

In Burgos, I started my first Camino in 2011 with Anna, whom I had met online shortly before. I had been nurturing the idea of walking the Camino de Santiago for several years but could not find anyone to join me. Until one day, a good friend advised me to go alone:

„My sister did it alone as well, and she also had concerns about her knee problems", he said.

So, I decided to go alone. After half a year of planning, with everything set two weeks before departure, Anna suddenly contacted me. She had read my post in a Camino forum and liked the idea of starting together. Within two days, we managed to get Anna a plane and bus ticket from Barcelona to Burgos, literally the last seats for the connections I had booked months in advance, and we looked forward to the adventure together.

After the almost 9-hour bus ride, which my restless legs syndrome turned into a real torment, we are now in Burgos and first go to the post office. The prices in Spain were a bit daunting for me back then due to currency conversion, so I had packed some Travellunches and 5-minute terrines just in case. Half of my food supplies, my Olympus camera, which I preferred to use over just my phone (Nokia C6) to photograph the cathedral in Santiago de Compostela, along with spare batteries, and a good blouse for visiting Saint James, now end up in a nice yellow box and are sent as ‚poste restante' to León.

Somewhat relieved, we now head to the cathedral, which unfortunately is already closed. But nearby is the municipal albergue, where we buy our Credenciale and get our first stamps. We treat ourselves to an ice cream in the beautiful Paseo del Espolón park near the Puente de Santa Maria, before retiring to our hotel room almost at the western end of the city.

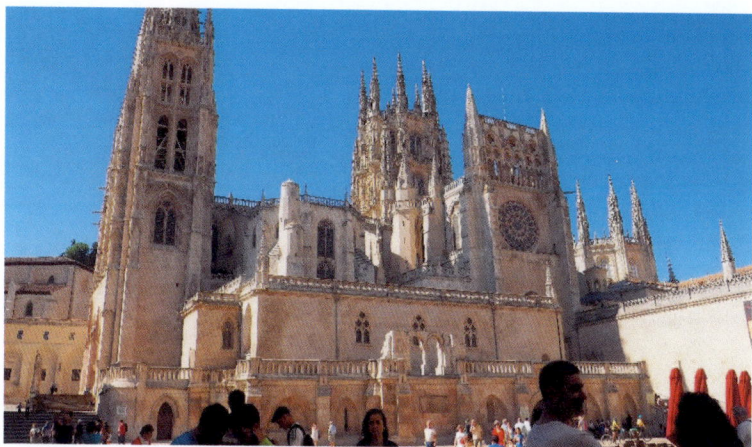

A few years later, I even got to attend a pontifical mass in the beautiful Burgos Cathedral with my mother. It's a sight I'll never forget: the interplay of colors in the slightly yellow-cream Gothic vault, with blue sky in the windows in between and the gold of the high altar, definitely belongs in the top ten of the most beautiful things I have seen in life.

„Una gran señal apareció en el cielo: una Mujer, vestida del sol, con la luna bajo sus pies, y una corona de doce estrellas sobre su cabeza" singt der Chor "A great sign appeared in the sky: a woman, clothed with the sun, with the moon under her feet, and a crown of twelve stars on her head" (Revelation 12:1).

The white lilies on the altar, their shine and fragrance, and the incense make this August morning – the Feast of the Assumption of Mary into Heaven – as heavenly as it can get here on earth. Churches and liturgy have always been designed to give people at least a glimpse of heavenly reality and the heavenly liturgy. The most beautiful things that nature and humanity create come together here as a reflection of what no eye has seen and no ear has heard.

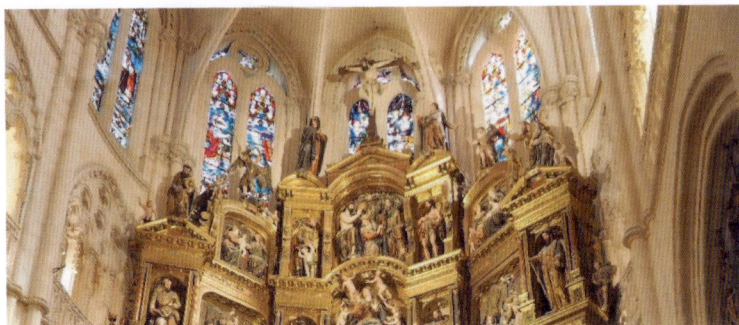

6.   Rabe de las Calzadas

In the small hotel in Burgos, we have breakfast without any rush. For the first day on the Camino de Santiago, we planned only 9 kilometers, a little warm-up to test the terrain, the shoes, and our own strength. The large cup of café con leche is just right. However, the two slices of toast with jam hardly deserve the name „breakfast" for a Central European, so I put a muesli bar in the side pocket of my backpack, just in case. On the other side, a full water bottle. We set off and promptly find the first metal scallop shells embedded in the sidewalk.

Outside the city, we meet many pilgrims on foot and on bicycles, all greeting us with „Hola!" and „Buen Camino!". In Tardajos, we take a short coffee break. The nice lady gives us two muffins as a gift.

Strengthened, we cover the last few kilometers at a good pace and soon stand in Rabe de las Calzadas in front of the still-closed albergue. So, we head to the small church, where it is shady and cool. I take the small donkey figure out of my pocket and place it on the bench next to me. I bought it last year at the Nuremberg Christmas market after reading a Camino book where a pilgrim walked the Camino with a (real) donkey. That book was my favorite of all the Camino books because it was the funniest, even though the author sometimes mocked Christianity a bit too harshly. Now I also have a donkey with me, albeit a small one. He looks at me with his big eyes, squinting, which always makes me smile. He also exudes a certain calmness, robustness, and humility; after all, Jesus entered Jerusalem on a donkey. I take a photo of my dusty hiking boots and my little companion. Later, I will chuckle at the first pilgrim photo, where my trouser legs are still neatly rolled up almost to measure.

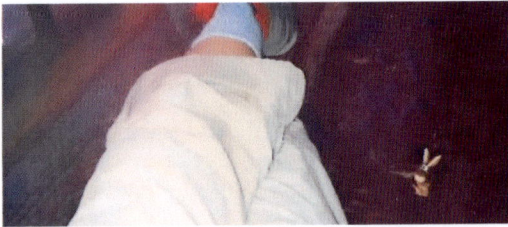

The albergue opens at one. Shoes and poles must stay in the entrance area. In the small, cozy dining room, we complete the formalities. The house reminds me of the retreat houses we used to go to in the summer. It feels good to be here. Upstairs, then a surprise. In the 8-bed room, male and female pilgrims are mixed. I look at Anna in surprise, but she takes it relaxed. For her, it's important that she can sleep on the bottom, so I climb onto the top bunk and take off my socks. Well, look at that – first day, first blister. I will carefully pierce it after the shower, disinfect it, and securely wrap it with a plaster. Through the window, equipped only with a mosquito net, you can see directly onto the small church. This village doesn't have much more to offer than the albergue and the church. There isn't even a store – one comes on wheels in the morning.

A few years ago, it was unimaginable for me to stay in an albergue with strangers. Here, however, I somehow feel safe. The room is silent. Most pilgrims go straight to sleep upon arrival, so the others behave as quietly as possible. It doesn't seem like anyone here plans to get drunk and run around, as in a youth hostel, so I breathe a sigh of relief and also fall asleep after a quick shower. We will eat something in the evening. The mixed dormitory still seems a bit odd to me, and, as it turns out later, there are indeed albergues (mostly private) in larger towns that offer separate sleeping rooms for men and women. I will look out for those. Before falling asleep, I remember the first report about the Camino de Santiago that I saw years ago on German television. The albergue there looked more like a garage covered with plastic sheeting. The sight gave me chills, yet the report sparked a desire in me to undertake this adventure. That seems to be the motto of my first Camino – facing my own fears. This also reminds me of my boss, who never uses the words „problem" or „difficulty," but always calls them „challenges."

In the evening, we eat our ready-made meals, which only need to be mixed with hot water, and then go to sleep again.

7.   Rabe de las Calzadas
at night

The church bells ring every 15 minutes, even at night, and at least two other pilgrims are snoring like an old tractor. It's impossible to block out. Additionally, my top bunk is directly opposite the small light above the door. Tired or not, it's just impossible to fall asleep like this. It's a good thing I dozed a bit in the afternoon. Still, to be fit, I need to sleep now. So, I grab my earbuds and put on a movie on my phone. This trick has worked many times before. With my favorite series, which I know well, I quickly switch off; it distracts my thoughts but isn't exciting enough to keep me awake. One episode is enough to send me off to dreamland.

8.   Hontanas

By 5 o'clock, the first pilgrims leave the albergue, quietly and in the dark. We start an hour later, after a leisurely breakfast of muesli from our backpacks and a good coffee from the hospitalera. In the dawn light, you have to pay close attention to not overlook the yellow arrows. The rising sun tinges the mist pink, and I regret that I can only capture this sight with my camera phone. It's still cool, and the sky is partly cloudy. Wonderful hiking weather.

Yesterday's first impression is confirmed today. Anna is clearly fitter than me. She's also a bit taller, so she probably moves faster. She'll need some patience with me. What can you say, a pilgrimage is a penance. I just let her go ahead, and we meet again at the next intersection. Then we walk together again, chatting and praying. „Give us this day our daily bread," actually not just bread, but above all a place to sleep. Our stages are relatively short, and yesterday we even arrived at the albergue too early, but that's going to change; we've planned around 20 km for each day. And we should make sure to get a bed on time. At least I can't just add another 5 or 10 kilometers if everything is already full and we'd have to look for another place.

After two hours of marching, we take a break in Hornillos del Camino. The local bocadillos with cheese are long, actually whole baguettes. We have one cut in half and devour it with an iced tea outside on red plastic chairs with beer advertising, opposite the church of San Roman.

Although the area is mostly flat, allowing us to see everything for miles, our destination for today – Hontanas – is hidden almost until the end behind the horizon. Only shortly before the village does the path go downhill, and then suddenly the church tower and the other buildings appear in front of us. It's been over 18 kilometers today, and now I'm glad to have a bed in the small albergue. There's both a bar and a kitchen for those who want to cook for themselves. There we find two pilgrims from Germany—Caroline and her friend. They're cooking pasta with tomato sauce. In the bar downstairs, we find a red wine for 2 €. After the experience in Barcelona, we look at the bottle somewhat skeptically. However, it turns out that a Vino de Casa for this price can indeed be a delight. We share the bottle in the kitchen with our German-speaking acquaintances.

9.   San Nicolas de Puente Fitero

We set off again before sunrise. The third day crisis is often mentioned, and indeed, my feet are already hurting after half an hour. Anna, on the other hand, is as fit as ever – just apparently quite annoyed by my slow pace. So, we decide to walk separately for a while. Fortunately, the path so far is flat, even slightly downhill. I meet up with Anna again at the picturesque ruins of the Monastery and Hospital of San Anton. Here, they treated patients who, as is suspected today, suffered from ergot poisoning. The Gothic arches, now somewhat purposelessly protruding over the path, radiate a certain sacredness, and we walk the final stretch to Castrojeriz together, praying the rosary aloud. In a small bar right next to the church, we treat ourselves to another large café au lait and a piece of cake before continuing on. Just before leaving the town, I encounter an old man who stops, takes my right hand in his hands, and blesses me.

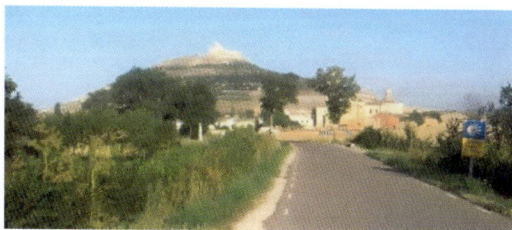

The most challenging part of today's stage is still ahead of us – a climb to the Meseta Pass. It's exhausting, but surprisingly, my feet hurt less here, at least while going uphill. And it's steep, a 150-meter ascent. At the top, there's a small hut, or rather a shelter, but unfortunately, no well, and my thoughts are now obsessively circling around cold drinks. Besides the small roof, there's no shade in sight, and there's no other option but to continue on between the endless fields. Eventually, we descend just as steeply and then back to flat terrain. The name Meseta comes, after all, from the word ‚mesa' – table. We're back on asphalt, and I'm slowly nearing tears. When a small pilgrim hostel, Ermita de San Nicolas, appears just before the famous Puente Fitero bridge, my decision is made – I'm not going a step further. The hospitalero on the bench is currently tending to the blisters of a young pilgrim. Dirk is from the Netherlands and is already on his way back from Santiago. He's walking the path without money, with his guitar, with which he earns what he needs along the way. Anna also gets her feet treated right away, securing us, as it turns out later, accommodation here. The small hostel with only 8 beds is intended only for pilgrims who wouldn't make it to the hostel in the village. Nonetheless, I keep my shoes on and will take care of them later myself. Accommodation, yes; hepatitis, no thanks.

The hostel used to be a chapel in the provincial wall. A group of Camino friends from Italy has now restored it and operates it as a small hostel. In the apse at the east end, there's a small altar with an icon triptych and a baptismal font. Otherwise, there's a small kitchenette, a long table, four bunk beds, and mattresses for the hospitaleros on the gallery. Electricity is only available in the small shack behind the hostel where the showers and toilets are located. Since today is Thursday, there's a foot washing before dinner. All pilgrims are asked to sit in the apse, the three hospitaleros currently on duty come in brown coats adorned with attached scallop shells. They kneel before each pilgrim one by one, say a blessing, and wash the pilgrim's feet, as Jesus did to the apostles at the Last Supper. Then we're invited to the table; dinner has also been prepared by the hospitaleros. There's pasta, salad, bread, wine, and fruit for dessert. Everyone shares a bit about themselves and their experiences on the Camino. Unfortunately, the older hospitalero doesn't speak English, so I try to refresh my little Italian, and surprisingly, it works well.

It's quite cold in the old walls at night, and I put my fleece T-shirt over my pajamas since my homemade lightweight sleeping bag is a bit too short to cover up to the neck.

Two gestures shape today—blessing and foot washing. I'm always amazed at how often people curse nowadays. I don't just mean swear words but how often in movies and daily life one person literally sends the other to hell. Such phrases have become almost commonplace for us, and most don't consider what they're actually saying. They probably don't mean it that way either. However, the devil cares little whether we meant it literally and exactly. He gladly comes when called, much more eagerly than we would like, and gladly takes advantage of every opportunity we give him to harm ourselves or others. Shouldn't we instead call upon God's help? "Bless those who persecute you; bless and do not curse them!" writes Paul to the Christians in Rome (Romans 12:14). Blessing is more than just good wishes. God is the one who blesses, meaning He bestows His graces upon us. When we bless, we not only wish good for others, but we ask God, who can fulfill these wishes, to do so. There was also something like a blessing in the foot washing

27

today. The hospitaleros prayed for each of us, asking that God and St. James accompany us on our pilgrimage. These words are also on the pilgrim passport. Blessing in the stricter sense, with laying on of hands and drawing the cross, is, however, bound to authority. Directly blessing, in representation of God, so to speak, is allowed by priests, parents to their children, the Mother Superior to the sisters of her community, and spouses to each other.

Foot washing itself is an expression of humility and love for one's neighbor. But this moment also reminds me of a verse from the book of Isaiah, which I'd like to translate literally from Latin here: "Quam pulchri super montes pedes annuntiantis, praedicantis pacem, annuntiantis bonum, praedicantis salutem, dicentis Sion: Regnavit Deus tuus!" - "How beautiful on the mountains are the feet of the messenger who brings good news, the good news of peace and salvation, the news that the God of Israel reigns!" (Isaiah 52:7). The pilgrim, by expressing their faith through their pilgrimage, is in a way proclaiming the good news. Their steps tell a story: God is mighty, God helps, He is worthy of our effort, He hears our persistent prayers. Or: I am a sinner and must atone for my misdeeds, but God is merciful, He looks upon my good intentions, my effort, and will forgive me. And those who were unable to undertake the pilgrimage themselves often tried to participate by caring for and supporting the pilgrim. Behind this lies not only the works of mercy that Jesus has entrusted to us but also the belief in the communion of saints, in our deep connection in Christ, in the understanding that the good deeds of one member of the mystical body of Christ benefit others as well.

As my thoughts continue to unravel, I try to fall asleep in the somewhat chilly room. Fortunately, tiredness eventually prevails.

10. Fromista

During the night, I made a rather unpleasant discovery. I wanted to use my rain jacket as an extra cover and was horrified to realize that I must have left it behind in the last hostel. Getting dressed and packing in the darkness can be challenging, and it's easy to overlook things. Although it hasn't rained yet, I should try to get a replacement as soon as possible.

After a quick breakfast, we set off. My feet are already hurting again. Soon, it feels just like yesterday, as if I have blistered feet, even though, by the way, I didn't have a single blister yesterday. I'm starting to doubt whether I'll be able to complete the whole journey. But even if I had to give up now, the evening yesterday was worth coming here for.

Today, the Camino first passes through fields of grain across the table-flat Meseta. From Boadilla onwards, fortunately, there is a bit more shade, and in parts, you walk directly along the Canal del Castilla. Fromista welcomes us with the sun-yellowed church of San Martin, one of the earliest examples of high Romanesque churches in Spain. It's a big surprise for me. Until now, when I thought of Romanesque, I pictured thick, bare, unadorned walls. Here, however, the cornice under the roof and around the window arches are adorned with a delicate pattern. The capitals around depict various motifs, and the different colors of sandstone form a decorative pattern. The interior of the church is almost empty. Apart from the decorative capitals, there are only three figures: Christ on the cross behind the simple stone altar, Saint Martin, and Saint James. We enjoy a brief respite from the heat in these old walls before heading to the pilgrim hostel, where we are greeted by full clotheslines in the courtyard. At the albergue, you can buy postcards from the hospitalero, but unfortunately, he doesn't have a rain poncho on offer. In the dormitory, I finally free my poor feet from the heavy hiking shoes and this time actually discover two blisters, albeit on the side of the heel and not where I suspected, between the toes. It doesn't make any sense. „Blister stitching" is supposedly better than simply piercing them. So this time, I actually leave a piece of thread as drainage in the blister and apply band-aids. Slipping into fresh socks and comfortable sandals, I set out in search of a replacement for my rain jacket.

As in every larger town along the way, I quickly find a store in Fromista that has everything a pilgrim's heart desires. A red rain poncho is quickly found. It's a poor substitute for my good jacket, and I actually hate hiking under such a plastic tent. But at the moment, I have no other choice. I hope the albergue in Hontanas responds to my email and my jacket somehow catches up with me. In the small store, there are all sorts of pilgrim gadgets: headgear, scallop shells, pins with yellow arrows, magnets, cups, and plenty of jewelry with various symbols, most of which come from New Age spirituality. A strange mix of religion and culture. I often wonder if some pilgrims actually know what they are wearing around their necks as good luck charms and the like. Lost in thought, I instinctively stroke my scapular medal. Many say that Catholic devotional items are also such talismans. There is indeed a certain similarity. In both cases, we are dealing with material objects that acquire spiritual significance. The huge difference, however, is to whom they are dedicated. If someone believes in the power of a talisman, they are actually believing in magic, which is nothing more than the realm of the adversary. Conversely, when a cross, medal, or candle is blessed, prayers are offered to God, asking Him to grant special graces to the person using, wearing, or praying with these objects. And God hears our prayers when we ask for something good. The medal itself has no power, but God can use this piece of matter; He blesses the one who wears this medal. Similarly, the evil one can use matter dedicated to him in some ritual or to which we attribute magical significance, thus opening a small door for him because we are sinning against the first commandment.

In Germany, there has been a real boom lately for „angel callers," and I am always tempted to ask the respective seller since when one needs a magical object for this purpose. After all, my guardian angel is always with me, and I can speak with him at any time. However, my Spanish would not be sufficient for such a discussion, so I pay for my rain poncho and a pack of bandaids and leave the store. On the way back to the hostel, I see patterns painted on the asphalt, most likely serving as stencils for flower carpets for the Corpus Christi procession two weeks ago. However, my thoughts are currently more focused on earthly sustenance. In a bar that entices me with a „free WiFi" sign, I order a bocadillo and a glass of white wine and add a few photos to my Camino blog. According to the comments, it is regularly read not only by my parents but also by some colleagues.

In the albergue, Anna sits on her bed with the pilgrim guidebook in hand. She wants to walk to Calzadilla de la Cueza tomorrow. A whopping 36 kilometers! My feet definitely won't handle that. The 19 to Carrion de los Condes are enough for me. After a short consideration, we decide to walk separately for the next few days and meet again on Wednesday in Leon, where our package is also waiting.

11. Carrion de los Condes

Today's route is, according to my guidebook, flat and comfortable. I decide to wear sandals. The risk of spraining my ankle on the straight paths is low, so it should be doable without high-cut shoes. I have to stop from time to time to shake out the small stones that get into my sandals, but this freedom is incredibly good for my feet. The soles of my feet still feel somewhat irritated, but the painful pressure from previous days is gone. I grab breakfast on the way at a bar – a chocolate croissant, a cup of cafe con leche, and orange juice. Sunflowers are blooming along the way, and rainbows adorn the irrigation systems.

The Camino here is wide and comfortable, almost two lanes wide, along the main road. One just has to be careful not to trip over the scallop shell stone that keeps appearing in the middle of the path. Before Revenga de Campos, I suddenly encounter a living obstacle. A flock of sheep occupies the entire width of the road and sidewalk. I let their calmness infect me and simply wait until they move a bit to the side. The sky is mercifully covered with some clouds today, so there's nothing forcing me to walk quickly. Fortunately, the sun is mostly covered today. However, there is another loss to report. Yesterday in the bathroom, I managed to break the sun attachment for my glasses in two halves. Although I tried to save it with super glue, whether it will hold up in the long run is doubtful. Many pilgrims describe the Meseta as the worst part of the Camino, but I enjoy it. At least in this weather, with a wide path and sunflower fields – this warm yellow has always been my favorite color, and I can't get enough of it now. I take a lunch break along the way. A piece of tortilla – potato omelet, a stuffed pepper with baguette, and a small beer strengthen me for the last few kilometers. A text message from Anna: „The path behind Carrion is unfortunately not suitable for sandals." She started much earlier than I did today and is already on my route for tomorrow. I hope my feet have recovered enough today and that I can put on my hiking shoes again tomorrow.

Just beyond Villarmentero de Campos is a rest area with a few benches and a sprinkler nozzle apparently for cooling off pilgrims. Arriving in Carrion, I leave my backpack in the hotel room and, after a quick shower, take a little tour through the city. At Monasterio Santa Clara, there is currently a rosary service. I can't say the Hail Mary in Spanish, but after a few minutes, I manage to distinguish the words of the sisters behind the grille and try to join in.

Later, there is a mass with a pilgrim blessing at the Church of Santa Maria del Camino. But first, I treat myself to a slice of pizza in a Cerveceria, which is actually like a beer bar and has the charm of a London pub. However, the food doesn't agree with me today, and instead of going directly to the church, I first walk back to my hotel room. My cousin calls such sensations the „pharaoh's revenge," but I doubt whether pharaohs currently rule in Spain or ever have.

I arrive slightly late for the mass and am a bit amazed. In Italy, thanks to my knowledge of Latin, I usually understood the sermons. Here, I'm somewhat lost. The mystery is revealed at the end. The priest admits to giving the sermon in the local dialect and now gives a summary for those who don't understand it. Now I actually understand him, mostly at least. Oddly enough, isn't the local language – Castilian – what we know as Spanish? Maybe there are gradations like between Franconian and Upper Palatinate... The priest talks about the different soils of our hearts on which the word of God falls. What kind of soil am I actually? Maybe not so stony. More like the piece of earth with many thistles that dampen the growth of the word – those are the worldly worries and fears, the selfishness that prevent me from doing God's will and following Him more decisively. Then there is a special pilgrim blessing.

Back at the hotel, I flip through the TV channels, unfortunately there is nothing in German and nothing interesting in general. So I go to bed soon and plan to start early in the morning. Shortly before my flight to Spain, I wondered if after years of dreaming of the Camino, reality might disappoint me. But no, the path is indeed arduous, physically and sometimes psychologically, but it is worth the effort. I am not disappointed. Every day is a new adventure, and even though getting up early is a struggle, once I'm on the way, I'm glad to have made it again.

12.   Calzadilla de la Cueza

This time, unfortunately, I didn't manage to get up early. Instead of starting at 6, I set off again at 8. However, Saint James seems to favor me, granting me a cloudy sky today as well. Luckily. Between Carrion de los Condes and Calzadilla de la Cueza, there's nothing at all. Nothing but fields. No shade, hardly any trees, no villages, not even a well or shelter for sun-battered pilgrims. So, the clouds are more than welcome. The journey is thus much more pleasant than in scorching heat. Nonetheless, this stage is boring. Actually, one could easily walk this stretch in sandals, I don't know why Anna warned me about it. Gray sky and beige fields, and even though you can see the path for kilometers ahead and behind, there are hardly any other people in sight. So, I listen to music from my phone to keep in rhythm. And then a fellow pilgrim catches up with me.

„You look pretty tired," she says, stopping beside me, seemingly assuming I speak German too.

„Yeah," I smile back, „I could really use a coffee and some ice cream right about now."

„When I need something, I just order it from the Universe," the stranger laughs.

„What do you mean?"

„I read about it in a book about the Camino. Give it a try," she quickens her pace again and disappears behind the next curve. Now I even remember which book she's referring to. One of the many about the Camino that I've read before, albeit with considerable skepticism and great bewilderment. No, I certainly won't be ordering anything from the Universe. The Universe, like me, is just God's creation and it doesn't listen. But I am a child of God, and the Father listens to me when I ask Him for something. He may not make ice cream fall from the sky – He's not a waiter whom I can snap my fingers at to order something – but He is my Father, and, well, a father doesn't always let his child have ice cream before lunch. Still, I trust in Him. I don't want superpowers that fulfill all my wishes; I'd rather be the child who doesn't have to understand everything, but relies on its Father. That's why I kneel when I go to Communion, because before God, I am His little child. And I open my mouth, like a baby being fed by its parents. *„Truly, I say to you, unless you turn and become like children, you will never enter the kingdom of heaven"* (Mt 18:3).

My grandma always used to say that music takes away all seven pains. I must have more than seven, because even my favorite songs only partially alleviate them. After a few kilometers, my feet in the hiking boots start to bother me again. At some point, I get the idea to give them a bit more room and remove the gel insole from one shoe. Lo and behold, the trick works. The insoles feel soft and comfortable, but apparently they're a bit too thick, and when my feet swell a bit while walking, they get pinched. At the next stop, I also take out the second insole and feel worlds better. The soles are a bit harder, but the thick hiking socks still provide enough cushioning, and I'm immensely relieved to have identified and eliminated the cause of my days-long suffering. The expensive insoles ceremoniously end up in a trash can. I just need to plan for a slightly shorter day tomorrow so my feet can fully recover, and then I can practically fly towards Santiago.

In Calzadilla, there's an albergue with a large courtyard and a swimming pool. But I'm too tired for swimming; a shower is enough for me. Under the shower, I wash my clothes and then collapse onto the bed. At the other end of the room, two girls are chatting in English. Suddenly, one of their phones rings, and she starts speaking Polish. I wait for the end of the call and introduce myself. Yes, the world is small. We arrange to meet later for a communal dinner.

In the small bar around the corner, Magda and I are joined by Sarah from Italy, as well as Jens and Tobias from Berlin. I'd prefer to switch to German right away, but we stick to English so everyone can participate in the conversation. „Con pan y vino se anda el Camino," they say in Spain – With bread and wine, you walk the Way. Bread as the most basic food and wine, since its alcohol content made it much safer than water, which wasn't always distinguishable from wastewater. The symbolism of the two is rich. Bread and wine, the everyday and the ceremonial, body and spirit, work and suffering. Before my thoughts wander too far, the food is served. And indeed: just like in Italy, bread is served at every meal here, and we also indulge in a good bottle of red wine for our conversation. The others are starting from Saint-Jean-Pied-de-Port, and after the beautiful Pyrenees, they find the Meseta dull and boring. Jens graduated from high school this year and isn't sure what he wants to do next. He's starting his gap year soon, but before that, he hopes to gain some life-changing insights from the Camino. Tobias wants to pick himself up and reorganize after a difficult crisis, which he doesn't want to go into detail about. And the girls just love hiking and wanted to have a slightly different vacation this time. Actually, just like me. We exchange phone numbers again, take a few more photos, and soon head back to the albergue. I only have 9 kilometers tomorrow, so my feet can properly regenerate. But the guys want to go at least as far as Sahagun, probably even further if the weather cooperates, so they'll try to get up early.

13.   Terradillos de los Templarios

Today, whole fields of sunflowers accompany me again. A Camino signpost even seems to direct me straight into one of those fields. However, I resist the temptation and simply enjoy the sight of this warm yellow expanse as far as the eye can see. Near Ledigos, I see a sign indicating „Burgos 111 kilometers." According to my pilgrim's guidebook, it was actually a tad more on the Camino – 114 kilometers. So, I've covered the first hundred kilometers. There are still four times as much to go.

An SMS pops up: „If you happen to come across a nice pilgrim's hat somewhere, my head circumference is 60 cm." I can't help but laugh. „Da simma dabei, dat ist prima," I reply immediately. I know Jan from a two-week retreat in Rome two years ago. Somehow, we ended up together there. While the others used the breaks for rest or prayer, we usually continued walking alone with a city guide in hand to see this or that artwork that wasn't on the program, like the Ecstasy of St. Teresa or Caravaggio's „The Calling of St. Matthew." During a detour to the Sant Agnes Basilica on Via Nomentana, we even climbed over the railing to touch the saint's coffin. On the last day, we added a tour of the Colosseum and Roman Forum in the midday heat, topped off with an Espresso Corretto (coffee with grappa) at Caffè Greco. One day, we started talking about World Youth Day in Cologne, which Jan attended, and from then on, „Da simma dabei" became our hit. By the way, Jan has been a seminarian for two years now. Honestly, I have some friends who have taken this path in life. Whether it's because we're on the same wavelength or I have a special sense for it, it's happened to me several times that someone I got along well with entered the seminary. A nun once told me, „God sends you these guys so you'll pray for them especially." On the other hand, my cousin jokes, „See, after they've met you, they'd rather become celibates." Great. Unfortunately, my great love once ended up on that list too.

In Germany, some friends pity me for studying theology in vain, since as a woman, I can't be ordained in the Catholic Church anyway. I never actually thought about wanting to be a priest. There are good reasons why women aren't ordained, and I'm glad about that. Take confession, for example. An important function of the confessor is to objectify the thoughts, sometimes doubts, of the penitent. Men are naturally much better at this. For example, if I were sitting in the confessional during PMS, woe to the poor penitent whom I would likely scold completely unjustly. Or during pregnancy, I might put up a sign: „For the next 9 months, only cheerful penitents, I'm already crying enough." Jokes aside. Contrary to some gossipers, of course, a woman can keep a secret, but she can at least talk about it with the friend who confided in her. Luckily, because women process information, feelings, and stress by talking about them. If they suddenly had the burden of a hundred penitents loaded onto them, they would break down, whereas a man can simply emotionally distance himself from what he's heard, and even if something burdens him, he usually doesn't feel the need to talk about it. A priest friend once told me that after hearing confessions for several hours (probably before Easter), he had to lie down with a headache and fever. I can't even imagine a woman in his place.

Speaking of priests, tonight I'm staying in Terradillos de los Templarios, and look at that, the hostel is called Jacques de Molay.

Actually, I could keep walking. My feet feel much better without the insoles. But this lovely hostel with nice 5-bed rooms, a terrace, and a cozy dining room is very tempting. And indeed, it turns out to be a nice evening. I share the room with Gerda from Switzerland and Julia from Freiburg. It turns out they're walking the same pace as me on the Camino; we've done exactly the same stages in the last few days. It's amazing that we haven't met until now. We decide to walk together tomorrow.

But now we want to try the local pilgrim's menu. It feels good to speak German again. In the dining room, Thomas from Kiel joins us right away. He notices my surprised look and explains to us immediately why his left calf is completely white, even though he otherwise has a healthy tan. Last year, he got deep vein thrombosis in that leg, and since then, he has to wear a support stocking. This illness, which threw him off his life path, is also, as he says, the reason why he's walking the Camino. And he's actually walking it from Kiel on foot. At least every other fellow pilgrim walks the Camino out of a crisis or after a traumatic experience, or because they're at a point where they have to make important decisions for the future. But before our conversation turns into group therapy, I talk about my semester abroad, which I spent in Kiel years ago. Thomas was studying there at the same time. But since he lived at home, we didn't run into each other. I spent most of my time either in the library or in the Botanical Garden right next door.

14. Sahagún

Somehow, I slept restlessly this time. A few times, I even woke up thinking someone had screamed. But I fell back asleep immediately and continued dreaming about my old love from my student days. It had been more than ten years since then, yet the memories kept coming back in dreams. A friend once told me that something similar often happens to her; she dreams of someone and wakes up at that moment. For her, it was a clear sign – her guardian angel woke her up so she could pray for that person who needed prayer at that moment. Saint Padre Pio often said to others: „If you need my help, send me your guardian angel." I've often asked my guardian angel too, for example, before a difficult conversation – please ‚fly' to the person I have to speak to tomorrow and whisper a kind word to them, prepare the ground for this conversation. Is my old friend currently going through difficulties and has sent me his guardian angel to wake me up and ask for prayer? Perhaps God simply wanted to remind me that I haven't prayed for this person in a long time? Or was it just my own subconscious telling me that I still haven't made peace with my past? The answer, I guess, I'll never know here on earth. But no matter what it is, I want to make the best of it – I offer the following day, all the efforts and difficulties, for this person.

And it's not an easy day. It started very strangely. We were supposed to start together as a group of three. But when I woke up, Gerda had already left the room, and Julia was still asleep. When I quietly asked her, she just waved me off and went back to sleep. So, I left her a note with my phone number

43

on the bedside table, got dressed, and set off. The whole situation is extremely strange. Did we have a fight in the night that I don't remember? Was I perhaps the one who screamed or said something in my sleep that offended the other? I would never find the answer to these questions, although years later I found one of the girls on Facebook and asked. But maybe some Camino acquaintances simply end with a bottle of wine in the evening.

The weather matches my melancholy mood too. It's drizzling from the start. I put on my pink rain poncho over myself and my backpack. But this makes walking even more difficult. The plastic flutters in the wind, and underneath, I sweat more with every step, and the rain becomes more intense over time. Just in the nick of time, I reach the Ermita de la Virgen del Puente in Valdaraduey before the morning drizzle turns into a veritable downpour. However, the small building is closed, and I can only stand as close to the wall as possible and hold the poncho over myself because the narrow overhang of the hermitage practically offers no protection from the raging elements. Well, I did want to offer the hardships of this day for someone, so I shouldn't be surprised that the day is anything but easy.

Fortunately, the downpour subsides after a short while, and I can continue my march. But the last 3 kilometers to Sahagun somehow seem endless. Everything looks brown-gray, the gray sky is reflected in the puddles, and I feel the first signs of a sinus infection. So, my first order of business in Sahagun is to look for a pharmacy and get a pack of aspirin. I show the lady my note with the translation of „tea tree oil" on it: „El aceite del árbol del té," but apparently, she doesn't have it in stock or doesn't know what I mean. I'll probably have to make do with the 2 ml I brought from home.

Actually, today I'm supposed to meet Anna in Leon. We even booked a room there, and our mail is waiting there too. Anna has already arrived at the small hostel; she sent me an SMS. But I'm still 50 kilometers away from León. I'll probably skip them with a train. It might even be better for my sinuses.

15.   León

On my way from the train station in León to the hostel, I tried
once again with the „árbol del té," and this time the friendly
pharmacist promised to get it for me tomorrow morning. At
least there's a glimmer of hope. Once in the room, Anna and
I exchanged stories of our experiences and encounters from
the last four days, which we had walked separately. My attempt
to send Anna to find the post office quickly failed, so despite
my runny nose, I went into the city. It turns out, however, that
it was only to face the next setback of the day. The post office
had already closed. Nevertheless, I managed to find a sports
shop on the way, where I quickly got myself a fleece pullover
and a rain jacket. Reading the outdoor temperature display with
horror, I saw it was 14 degrees Celsius. In Spain... In the middle
of July... I couldn't even think about sightseeing in the city at
the moment. At the reception, I got myself a cup of hot water
and tried to tackle my cold with tea tree oil inhalation.

16. Virgen del Camino

Despite the somewhat tense atmosphere last night, we set off together with a small detour to my pharmacy and the post office. The one that was closed yesterday, by the way, wasn't even the right one. So, first, we need to find the main post office of the city, queue up in the correspondingly long (main) line there until we get to our package sent from Burgos. Along with the second half of the food supplies, from today onwards, I'll also be carrying my camera again – I'm looking forward to the additional 400 g. Why didn't I send it directly to Santiago? After all, I take photos on the way with my phone because I want to save the camera batteries for the cathedral. However, out of sheer joy at this reunion with the contents of my package, I at least manage to snap a photo of Gaudi's famous Casa de los Botines with the camera. Quickly as I pass by... Unfortunately, I won't be able to visit the beautiful Cathedral of León. Although we only planned 8 kilometers for today, the post visit makes us start from León quite late. The sun is already beating down on us, and despite the comfortable sidewalk, the constantly uphill path is relatively strenuous. Or am I sick after all?

The albergue in Virgen del Camino is quite large and comfortable. There's a big dining room with a modern kitchen, where I discover coffee varieties from a vending machine that I've never heard of. A three-person Polish-speaking family is cooking in the kitchen. We strike up a conversation. They are traveling without sleeping bags because they relied on there being blankets in every hostel. Unfortunately, that wasn't the case everywhere, and by now, the man has caught a pretty nasty cold. He even went to the doctor here in Spain and was prescribed an antibiotic. The woman is cooking spaghetti, and I'm invited to join them for dinner. However, I'm already in the process of preparing my „dry food" – the aliophylized potato-leek pot with ham. At least, this means I'll have 125 g less to carry tomorrow. I take my aspirin and fall into bed.

Three hours later, I'm awakened by Anna, who has been washing and exploring the area in the meantime. She's quite shocked to see me sleeping so much during the day. Apparently, I'm sicker than she thought. But after the aspirin and my „nap," I'm feeling somewhat better. Now I can do my laundry. What was that saying again? „You always meet twice in life." Whether it's true in life, I don't know, but on the Camino de

Santiago, it certainly seems to be the case. Walking past the door of the men's restroom, I suddenly think I see a familiar face. And indeed, a little later, I run into Thomas from Kiel in the kitchen, with whom we spent a nice evening in Terradillos with Gerda and Julia the day before yesterday. Thomas is surprised that I seem to have caught up with him, as I claimed not to walk 20 km a day. I confess my little cheat, and we exchange phone numbers in case we should happen to end up in the same place at the same time again.

In the afternoon, the sun shines directly into the windows in the sloping roof of the sleeping area, highlighting all the disadvantages of this low, barracks-like building. Apparently, no one thought about proper air circulation, especially not with the crowd sleeping here in a relatively small space. Consequently, the air at night becomes stuffy, and it doesn't really cool down. Just yesterday, I complained about the measly 14 degrees outside, but today it feels like 34 in this greenhouse. Nevertheless, I realize that I prefer to sleep in the pilgrim hostels. Last night, in the small room, I missed the other pilgrims

17.   Hospital de Orbigo

Ha! This time, I got up before Anna and got ready. The hostel is still closed, and it's still pitch dark outside. So, I leisurely enjoy my coffee and a few cookies before we can start walking. The air outside is cool and dry, and after just a few meters, my sinuses start acting up. Every breath feels like fire in my nose. On the other hand, it's too cold to breathe through my mouth, so I hold a tissue to my face. The slightly moister air collected underneath brings some relief. But the mood is already ruined. Today, the path mostly follows the main road, first for kilometers on asphalt and then on a sandy trail overgrown with bushes from both sides, barely enough room to pass through. I let Anna walk ahead and trudge along, full of anger towards the world, the Camino, my sinuses, the sun, which always burns on the Camino from the same side, first from behind and then around noon from the left.

No, I don't want to remember this stage, I just want to forget these 28 kilometers. They say about the Camino that it eventually brings everyone to tears. Whether my current suffering is what they mean, I doubt it.

Arriving in Hospital de Orbigo, I should actually admire the famous bridge – Puente Passo Honroso – but that's absolutely not possible today. The bridge is made of stones. It's not paved; it's made of stones of different shapes that feel like shards of glass to my battered feet, even though I'm wearing shoes, of course. Now I'm angry at the bridge too. I put one foot in front of the other and try not to scream each time. The sides of the bridge are covered with scaffolding and nets, so I'm actually not missing anything. In the village itself, fortunately, the pedestrian path is made of flat granite slabs. I eventually make it to the Albergue Paroquial, where Anna is already waiting for me. I get my stamp and a bed. The albergue consists of a main building with a courtyard and an additional wing that extends into the garden, where more dormitories are located. On one of the ceiling beams, there's the phrase „El turista exige, el peregrino agradece" – The tourist demands, the pilgrim is grateful. Today, gratitude isn't really working for me. Although, I am grateful somehow to have made it here and to be rid of my shoes now. Even without insoles, my feet are reaching their limits with this number of kilometers.

However, the walking is not over for today. I urgently need a pharmacy. Fortunately, it's only 300 m away. According to Wikipedia, Spaniards use the Latin word „Sinusitis" for sinusitis. Armed with this knowledge, I'm ready for my mission. The kind lady at the pharmacy gives me a packet of expectorant powder right away. If only I had looked up the word for nasal drops too. I have no choice but to gesture to her what I actually need. She understands me immediately and also gives me nasal spray. By the way, I also take the powder with me. Next to the pharmacy, there's also a shop, and since today is my father's birthday, I buy myself some donuts and a non-alcoholic beer.

Before falling asleep, a slogan for the Camino comes to mind
– Camino connecting people!

18.   Ponferrada

In the night, it's quite damp and cold in the dormitory. Can't seem to please me, can they? No, definitely not today. My body unequivocally tells me that I've reached its limits. I must listen to it, or I'll soon become unbearable for others. So, I quickly tell the early-rising Anna that I need a break and will take a bus ride for a stretch. We'll figure out where and when to meet later on the phone. However, I get up shortly afterward because the dampness is becoming really uncomfortable. After breakfast, I sit down at the computer and check the bus schedules. The selection isn't extensive, but Ponferrada as the next destination doesn't sound bad. I find a small hotel in the old town and book a room with a private bathroom for the next two nights.

The bus stop is quickly found, but the bus itself takes its time. After 15 minutes, I'm almost giving up when it finally arrives.

Despite this decision seeming like the right one, I'm still in the bus with a bad mood and somehow a guilty conscience. The beautiful landscape with green hills beyond the window and the pilgrims, some of whom are walking parallel to the bus route, don't make it any easier for me. I'd much rather be out there. The special atmosphere of the first days on the Camino somehow seems to have vanished. Also, thoughts about how to plan the remaining stages to somehow keep up with Anna are becoming more and more annoying. Our walking paces simply don't match. While I'm relieved to finally arrive at an albergie by noon and lay down, Anna complains that we've arrived so early again, and what is she supposed to do here for half the day... With every kilometer, the decision to walk the path alone matures within me. I'd spare myself the stress of trailing after her, and she wouldn't have to slow down her pace because of me... Even before the bus stops in Ponferrada, the decision is made, and I send Anna a text message.

Somehow, the situation reminds me of many others in my life. Yes, even the college love I dreamt about three days ago. We often have a very clear idea of what would make us happy, and we cling to that idea. This time, it was the concept that it's better to walk the Camino together. Probably, there was also a lot of fear behind it. Fortunately, in this case, my own body showed me the yellow card. But when strong emotions come into play, our judgment is much more impaired. It can quickly happen that we bend not just for a few days, but even for years, just to not lose this supposed happiness. Then, often not even voices of reason from outside can penetrate us, telling us that our concept of happiness actually doesn't do us any good. How many people are stuck in destructive relationships without wanting to admit it? How often do we pursue a career goal without questioning it?

But what if not only the health of the body or mind is at stake, but much more? The body quickly signals when something is wrong. The mind eventually says: „Stop." However, the voice of our conscience is much quieter, and when it says something uncomfortable, we often quickly silence it. Unfortunately, not to our benefit. Most likely, at some point in our lives, our feelings have told us that we would be so happy with the married colleague or neighbor. And if the colleague or neighbor also feels the same, then is our conscience still loud enough that we can trust God that He wants something better for us with His commandments than our clouded judgment? No, my college love back then wasn't married. And to this day, I'm not really sure why it didn't work out back then. But somehow, I trust that it was better this way, that I didn't get what I wanted. The father knows why He doesn't let the child eat the beautiful red toadstool. We understand some parental prohibitions over the years, but others we will probably only see clearly in heaven.

From the bus station in Ponferrada to the medieval center, it's quite a climb, and suddenly I feel my left Achilles tendon. However, the hotel is soon found, next to the picturesque Torre del Reloj (Clock Tower). In the basement, there's a small restaurant, and I immediately order a pilgrim's menu: a vegetable salad with mayo, fish with potatoes, and caramel pudding from a plastic cup. With red wine. I'll probably never get used to red wine with fish, but apparently, the Spaniards don't have white wine. I ask the waiter for the Wi-Fi password.

„¿Tienes ordenador?" he asks somewhat surprised.

„Si"

He repeats the question. Either he doubts my Spanish skills or he doesn't know yet that there are already internet-capable phones, and the idea of a pilgrim with a „ordenador" in the backpack logically seems absurd to him. But now, an email from the hostel in Hontanas appears on my internet-capable phone, confirming that my rain jacket has indeed been found and can be sent to me.

Before I go to bed, I quickly go shopping. For my garlic remedy, which is supposed to wipe out all unwanted microbes in my sinuses, I need a yogurt. The white one looks like plain yogurt, so I grab it. However, back in the room, there's a nasty surprise. I won't describe the taste mixture of vanilla yogurt, garlic, and Salzgurken-water (cucumbers preserved with salt and lacto-fermentation, similar to sauerkraut) here. I quickly swallow it down and rinse with a generous amount of water. The medieval pilgrims surely ate worse, but as Mario in San Nicolas said, we're pilgrims, not martyrs. Yes, those who can read (even in foreign languages) are clearly at an advantage. I take a long, hot shower – nothing soothes the sinuses like a steam bath – and sleep through the rest of the day.

19.   Ponferrada day 2.

The following day, I spend most of my time in bed. Besides that, I take two more steam showers, and at noon, I treat myself to a Quatro Staggione pizza and visit the castle. For the second time on the Camino, I encounter the Templars, the knightly order surrounded by most legends and mysteries. The papal investigation at the time deemed the heresy accusations unfounded, yet the Pope dissolved the order due to the bad reputation resulting from the royal trial, which was actually about the king wanting access to the order's treasure. In modern times, other knightly orders were also turned into shame for church history. However, the knightly orders in Europe were no less significant for civilization than, for example, the Cistercians. They built roads, schools, hospitals, breweries, and the architecture of these areas is still a clear testament to their work. I understand that not everything was always above board, but just like there are bad teachers and yet no one questions the school as a whole.

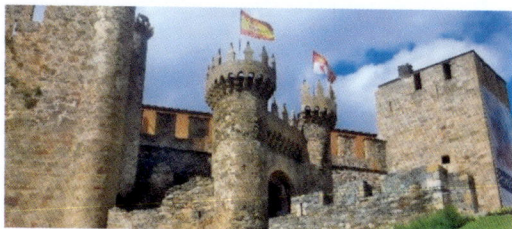

The castle in Ponferrada is impressive. Outside, I encounter a small procession with the figure of Saint Roch. That's also a reunion, and as soon as I'm back on the hotel Wi-Fi, I'll actually do some research on what the bloody knees and the dog are all about. Surprisingly, despite the scallop shells on his clothing, Rochus has almost nothing to do with the Camino. Except for the fact that he was a pilgrim. However, he journeyed from Montpellier to Rome, taking care of plague victims and falling ill himself. During the illness, which he spent in a forest hut, he was provided with bread by a dog until he recovered.

Anna wants to be in Santiago on July 24th. She hasn't written what she plans to do there until her return flight on August 3rd. I prefer to stick to my comfortable pace. Tomorrow, I'll see if my Achilles tendon gives me some rest and if I can start walking again. Thanks to my massive attack, the sinus infection has subsided.

20. Cacabelos

And I'm on the road again.

The Camino is like life in miniature. There are different stages. Some you breeze through, others you crawl through almost on all fours. Sometimes you walk alone, then again in company, perhaps with someone who has a better overview. Because some signposts you can see from afar, others you have to search for painstakingly, and sometimes you completely overlook the yellow arrow and make a painful detour. Somehow, you have to find a middle ground so that you keep an eye on the path and don't stumble over a stone, but at the same time, you don't miss the beautiful landscape while just looking at your feet. Well then: *Ultreia, et Suseia, Deus, adjuva nos!*

Shortly after Ponferrada in Fuentas Nuevas, I find a Holy Mass. A half-hour one... On Sunday...

I've definitely left the Meseta behind. It ended already before Astorga, but I missed these mountains.

In Cacabelos, there's a whole new kind of albergue. Around the church, a row of mini bungalows with two beds each has been built into the wall around the church square. I share my double room with Heidi from Switzerland. She's already on her way back from Santiago and has been on the road for 3.5 months. Unfortunately, the hostel doesn't have a kitchen, only a vending machine, but there's no hot water in it. So, I have no choice but to go out to eat.

On the way, I meet a pilgrim couple who ask me about the local albergue in English. Somehow, their accent sounds familiar, so I ask if they speak German. Indeed. Well then, we can make it easier ;)

I embark on an adventure and try the local specialty – octopus. At that time, I'm still living outside the Eurozone and earning the equivalent of about 400€ per month. So, 16.50€ is a proud price for me. Is the dish worth it? Well, let's say: I suspect that in pre-Columbian times, you had to pay a lot more for the amount of salt and paprika in it. So, I can't really say what the octopus itself tastes like. Just like I can't say what snails taste like because they just taste like garlic butter to me. All in all, it was an interesting experience. And I end the pleasant afternoon in the cool room with a cafe con leche.

This morning, I found out that the ointment Anna left me with is not anti-inflammatory, but only promotes blood circulation. No wonder it didn't relieve my Achilles tendon pain. Tomorrow I'll buy Voltaren just in case.

In the night, I realize that the double rooms are actually connected under the roof, and thus you can hear the snoring of all 50 or 100 pilgrims.

21.   Portela de Valcarce

The next stages are a bit challenging to divide, so today I'll skip a few kilometers by bus – to Villafranca del Bierzo. Last time, I promise. From Villafranca, I start walking. The path along the busy road is actually a nightmare in parts, despite the pilgrim route now being separated from the road by a small concrete barrier. However, the weather is mild, and the surrounding mountains are beautiful. After 10 kilometers, I take a lunch break in Trabadelo and encounter my German acquaintances from El Puntido in Hontanas. As they say, you always meet twice. They're staying here for the night because the man also has tendon pain. Well, the word ‚also' isn't quite accurate. After the Voltaren treatment, my Achilles tendon is quiet, so I continue walking. It reminds me of an old joke: After we were connected to the power grid, the TV picture also improved significantly ;) .

However, upon my arrival in Portela, I discover three new blisters on my feet. Strange creatures. One would think that since they originate from uncomfortable spots in my shoes, they would reoccur in the same places. Far from it. My blisters always find new spots to spread to.

Anna arrived in O'Cebreiro today. According to her text message, the ascent was very strenuous. And once again, I'm tempted to skip ahead to save energy for the last 100 kilometers. Another text: „What do you want with the last 100 kilometers if you skip the most beautiful stages? You've planned this for so long, and now you're giving up? What will you have left? A pilgrim's passport with bar stamps?" Hello? Seriously? Achieving the goal is just as important as the journey. Sure, I'm eager to see the beautiful mountains, but what good are they if I'm so exhausted afterward that I can only fly home? She was the one who said the ascent was extremely difficult, even though she's much fitter than I am. That was the last exchange of text messages between us. That's why I'm now walking the path alone. Just like in life, everyone on the Camino must make their own decisions and stand by them. And just like in life – what good is the best fun on the way if it jeopardizes my ultimate goal – eternal life?

22.   La Laguna

I didn't manage to get up early again. However, but I'm determined to attempt the ascent to O Cebreiro, split over two days though. It's gray and foggy outside. According to the TV report, temperatures back home are currently twice as high as here. The internet promises ‚Lluvia débil' between 9 and 3 o'clock. That doesn't sound particularly good, but the automatic translation as ‚Lighten rain' sounds even worse, both grammatically and in terms of weather. Tomorrow, it's supposed to be nice for the second half of the ascent. Lucky me. I take a look at the comments on my blog. *„ Walking with your soul on your shoulder – that's not good. But with someone else's soul? Probably more reassuring, because there's someone to talk to :) So it's decided: tomorrow I'm walking with you! Will you allow me to sit on your left shoulder? You're probably still fidgeting with your right hand, I might fall off! You'll see how interesting tomorrow will be! I wonder if you're already guessing whose soul you'll be carrying?"* – unsigned. I indeed wonder who that is. Probably another sleepyhead like me.

I start walking, and after a few steps, I suddenly hear behind me:

„Angelus Domini nuntiavit Mariae."
"Et concepit de Spiritu Sancto."
"Ave Maria, gratia plena ..."

sung... in Latin... No, it's not my hitchhiker from the comment ;) Shortly after, three guys in cassocks overtake me, and I quietly join in the prayer. Interesting. That's what I call a good start to the day. After the young priests or seminarians have disappeared from earshot, I take out my phone and play the "Hours in honor of the Archangel Michael". Michael is one of my favorite saints, probably because I was baptized in a church named after him.

So far, there's no sign of the light rain, quite the opposite, it's even sunny. I look somewhat surprised at the road, which runs over me on several-meter-high stilts. I have to take a photo of the sight and send it to my father. Somehow, I'm glad to walk down here. Although up there, you surely don't have to watch out for cow pats. I take a short break in Herreiros. The lady asks where I'm from and if it's cold there. I just deny it, as my Spanish isn't good enough to explain to her that it's currently much hotter at home.

On the other hand, I notice that this humid mountain climate is much better for my sinuses than the dry heat on the Meseta.

I meet the three guys in cassocks again in La Faba, and we start talking. They're from the Fraternity of St. Peter from the United States. They're very surprised that I know the Fraternity. Unfortunately, they're still seminarians, so my hope of attending a „Tridentine" Mass is dashed. We all find the albergue in La Faba a bit too new-agey, so we continue walking, engrossed in conversation.

In the next village – La Laguna – I decide to stay, but the guys want to make it to O'Cebreiro today. In the albergue, I first order garlic soup and tortilla. By the way, the bread has been like ours for a few days – with sourdough and some rye. Until recently, there were only French baguettes. There's also cider here (and by that, I mean apple beer and not wine). Yesterday, I even came across a strawberry variety. On the road, rust-brown cows amble slowly and seemingly unsupervised. They seem to know the way to the pasture and back home by heart.

The dormitory is mixed again this time, and I think of what one of the seminarians said. They usually sleep in tents to avoid giving offense by sleeping with women in the same room. Strangely, I find that most people nowadays wouldn't be offended by it. No... Just as if he had sensed what I was thinking, a male fellow pilgrim comes out of the bathroom, wrapped only in a towel, and starts getting dressed in the dormitory, regardless of the fact that I'm sitting on the neighboring bed. Next to me is a pilgrim from Germany, and since the free-spirited man seems to be Spanish, I address the lady in German on the topic.

„It doesn't bother me", she says somewhat surprised „On the Camino, we're not male or female, just pilgrims. Nakedness isn't automatically something erotic".

Seriously? Have we reached the point where we're indifferent to the naked body? At least I haven't, even though I don't find this thick older fellow pilgrim particularly appealing. But maybe many people are indeed unfazed by it now. But that would mean we need ever stronger stimuli. And of course, the erotica and porn industry would be delighted.

The seminarian's words are like a thorn in my conscience. Of course, I understand that it's difficult to separate the rooms by gender in the albergues. You never know what the composition of the crowd will be on any given day. So, should a pilgrim who can't go any further be turned away just because the only available bed is in the wrong dormitory? However, on the rest of the way, I'll try to find women's dormitories.

23.   Triacastela

Yesterday I treated myself to the luxury of a washing machine and dryer. It costs a few euros, but the next morning, you don't have to pack semi-damp clothes. Do we still have anything in common with medieval pilgrims with all these conveniences? Or are we already so-called „turigrinos"?

According to the guidebook – I don't remember the edition, as I left the covers at home for weight reasons – there are still 165 km to Santiago. If I manage the ascent halfway, the rest will be a piece of cake. The fact is, at least yesterday, I didn't see anything worth discussing with Anna. The mountains are, of course, beautiful, and I absolutely enjoy them. I've always felt like a fish in water in the mountains. However, I don't notice any significant difference between this area and what I have just a few kilometers from home. That's why I don't need to fly to Spain. Therefore, the mountains are not my priority. But I continue walking, hoping that I have enough strength for both. I set off without setting a destination for today. I start to feel like sailors who leave the „destination port" column blank in the logbook until they drop anchor :)

The morning sun and the fresh mountain air are pure bliss. Slowly, mist slides down the slopes, causing me to walk under veils of clouds. In other places, the light disperses in the form of a rainbow – just in white. Dewdrops glisten in the spider-webs like crystals. I walk very slowly, savoring the heavenly sight. The effort of the ascent is definitely paying off now. On O'Cebreiro, you have to climb in the morning freshness just like this.

At the top, the fog is a bit thicker, giving the place a mystical atmosphere. In this small, high-altitude village church, a Eucharistic miracle occurred on Christmas in 1300. To the disappointment of the doubting monk, despite the snowstorm, a single farmer attended the Christmas Mass. And as the monk felt compelled to celebrate the Holy Mass, bread and wine visibly transformed into flesh and blood before his eyes (more on this in the last chapter). In recent years, there has been an increase in such miracles again, which surely correlates with growing doubts about the Eucharist. Interestingly, at least where such investigations have been conducted, the blood of the miracles has been found to have blood type AB, just like the blood on the Shroud of Turin, a blood type possessed by only 5% of the population. Coincidence?

I remember the three seminarians from yesterday. Saying that I know the Priestly Fraternity of St. Peter was actually overstating it. I was familiar with them, but until then, before my first Camino, I had not had any contact with them. I grew up with the post-conciliar Mass and just a few years ago, I was jumping around in church with teenagers with an electric guitar. It was only after my later move to Austria and then to Germany that I got to know the so-called „old" Mass, as it was uniformly introduced for the Roman Church at the Council of Trent. After experiencing the worst nightmares in the new Mass in Germany, such as an altar server who simply spilled the corporal onto the carpet after Mass, from which, despite my poor eyesight, I could pick up the clearly visible particles of the Body of Christ, I came to appreciate the „Tridentine" Mass even more and attend it as often as possible.

I have no idea whether I've become fitter and more accustomed to the backpack by now, or if it's the influence of the mountains, but walking feels particularly easy for me today. In Hospital de la Condensa, I only have a cider and continue walking. There are still 15 km to Triacastela, and it even seems doable to me. Along the way, I strike up a conversation with Susan from England, and we continue walking together. We pass by some albergues that don't really appeal to us. In the late afternoon, we actually arrive in Triacastela – after 25 kilometers, and that's through the mountains. I can only marvel. Less surprising is that the albergues are completely full at this time. However, the hospitalera offers us a double room in her home for €16 per person. What else can we do?

24. Samos

Susan with another girl and two guys from Denmark started in the morning. They plan to reach Sarria today, and since many pilgrims start the Camino there to complete the final 100 km, the demand for albergues is accordingly high. I'm taking a detour today. The Benedictine abbey in Samos is said to be worth a few extra kilometers. I'll only go to Sarria tomorrow, and as a precaution, I've booked a room there.

Last night, we were all sitting in the kitchen, and one of the guys was joking about the Spanish kilometers. Apparently, they are significantly longer than those we are familiar with from other countries. There must be something to it. Yesterday, on the way to Triacastela, we kept seeing signs that said „Triactastela 3 km." Those were apparently the longest three kilometers in the universe. Nevertheless, today I can't shake the impression that yesterday's 25 km felt much shorter than today's 9, which felt like at least 19. The detour to Samos leads pretty much through no man's land. The area is green, mostly walking through the forest, with small streams and bridges over them. Passing through small villages where there isn't even a vending machine, let alone a bar. The only attraction along the way is a new type of cemetery. I wonder if people will find it easier to get out of those graves during the resurrection than ours?

I first catch sight of the abbey from above before I actually arrive there. Unfortunately, the albergue is still closed, backpacks lined up neatly outside the door, and at this hour, the bar across the street only offers coffee and biscuits. On the Camino, you learn a lot about yourself. For example, I never thought I could examine my foot soles up close until I had to take care of blisters. Or that you can dry yourself off with two tissues after a shower if you forget your towel in the dormitory.

My faithful companion – the small clay donkey from the Nuremberg Christkindlesmarkt – encounters its larger counterpart today. Somehow, the Camino wouldn't be complete for me without a donkey.

In the afternoon, I participate in the monastery tour and then stay in the monastery church for Vespers and Holy Mass. Monastic life has fascinated me my whole life – the structured daily routine dictated by the Breviary hours and the Benedictine balance between ‚ora‘ and ‚labora.‘ I've always longed for it, but I can‘t seem to manage it in my everyday life. For centuries, these monasteries have radiated not only a spiritual atmosphere but also knowledge and civilization.

25. Sarria

Day by day, you feel less of the pilgrim atmosphere that impressed me so much at the beginning. There are more and more young people and families with children on the way, who simply see it as an affordable vacation. Where else can you get accommodation for 3 euros per person? In the hostels, it's now loud day and night. I've read in many reports that pilgrims who have already covered a few hundred kilometers experience a kind of culture shock here on the final stretch, and that veterans recognize each other by the noise level. After eleven o'clock, I approached the three Spaniards who were still loudly talking. In response, they moved their conversation to the very acoustic bathroom, which didn't improve the situation. This morning, they were reprimanded by a lady in Spanish. But what can you expect when even the hospitaleros were loudly chatting late into the night.

The weather is great, but the day starts with a mishap. After a few hundred meters, I realize that I've forgotten my hiking poles for the third time at breakfast in the bar. One might think I don't need them if I keep leaving them behind. But in fact, I soon notice that something is wrong, and walking becomes a bit harder. I need to attach a leash to them. Or teach them to bark ;)

Most of the time, I keep passing a Japanese pilgrim. When I take a break to check something in the guidebook or take a sip of water, he overtakes me, but shortly after, I catch up with him again. From Samos to Sarria, it's only 11 km, a bit more than yesterday, but somehow I'm faster today, and the kilometers fly by without feeling burdensome, even though there's no bar or rest area along the way again today. On the detour, the pilgrim infrastructure isn't as developed as on the main route. On the last kilometer, I met the Polish woman from Warsaw again, with whom I enjoyed dinner yesterday on the hill opposite the abbey. Most pilgrims gathered on the meadow there for a kind of picnic in the sunset.

During lunchtime, I arrive in Sarria and admire my latest blister growth in my single room. It doesn't look good. I puncture the large blister and apply bandages. Bandages are actually a good keyword; I should buy some. After the siesta, I head to the nearest pharmacy. Thankfully, yellow arrows on the floor lead directly from the door to the stand with the bandages. The owner seems to know very well what most pilgrims need. I make my purchase. Later in the room, I discover a small gift in the package – a mini backpack, which I've since been wearing in front for items needed on the go, such as the pilgrim passport. I end the evening in a pizzeria

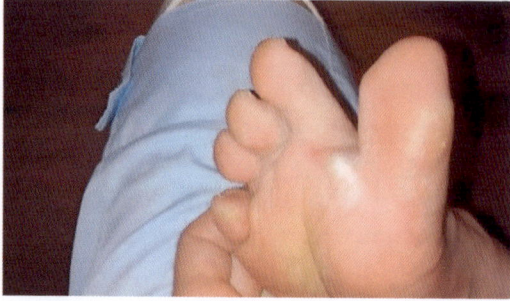

26.   the 100-kilometer stone

Back in 2011, I swore never to walk the last 100 kilometers again. As life goes, however, things always turn out differently than one expects. Just three years later, I found myself on the road from Sarria again, this time with my mother. And, as one might suspect, I've now even been on this final stretch of the Camino Frances for the third time, and slowly but surely, I'm developing a kind of love-hate relationship with this route.

2014 we flew from Vienna to Madrid and then took a train to Sarria. The landscape outside the train window looked desolately desert-like in parts, and the sight of the green forests and hills of Galicia afterwards felt like paradise. This time, we stayed in the monastery hostel right on the way.

And here I am at what is probably the most important milestone of the entire Camino de Santiago. From my destination, I am now just an hour's drive away. In the small bar behind the hundred-kilometer stone, I treat myself to a light lunch. Instead

of Tortilla de patatas, there is now Empanada gallega everywhere – a kind of large pastry filled with tuna. Of course,
a Café con leche is a must as well. The last hundred kilometers
have become famous because of the Compostela diploma that
one receives if they can prove at least this stretch through
stamps in the pilgrim's passport.

In jubilee years, on the other hand, visiting the Apostle's
tomb is associated with a plenary indulgence. However, nowadays, few people understand what it entails. Aside from many
associating the term solely with indulgence trading, I am dis-
mayed to find that even on many Camino de Santiago websites,
there is complete nonsense written about this topic. With an
indulgence, it is not about the remission of sins, but of
punishments. Sins are forgiven by God in the sacrament of
penance; one does not need to undertake a pilgrimage or per-
form any other indulgence works for that, just sincere repen-
tance and confession with a good intention. However, every
sin also incurs punishment. It can be likened to a vase that
broke while playing football in the living room. The child
regrets the game, and the mother quickly forgives it. However,
the fact remains that the vase remains broken. Every sin leaves
damages, even if the guilt has been forgiven. (More details
about it in last chapter of my first book „*Two cats on the
Camino*") These damages must be rectified as much as possible,
directly (returning what was stolen, retracting slander, etc.).
The rest can be offset through suffering, fasting, prayer, alms-
giving, good works, or ultimately in purgatory. An indulgence
is akin to a clearance sale. Since we, as the Church, form one
Body of Christ, there is an exchange of spiritual goods among
us all. Every sin leaves wounds on this body. However, the
Church's treasury contains countless merits of its saints, from
which we can draw at a low cost. They are like an elder brother
who almost freely replaces the precious vase for us. With
a plenary indulgence, we can eliminate all accumulated penal-
ties for sins already forgiven in confession, instead of through

many years of effort, simply through a religious act, such as a half-hour contemplation of the Rosary or visiting a Jubilee church. One must fulfill only 5 conditions for this:
1. sacramental confession and state of grace,
2. Holy Communion,
3. inner freedom from any attachment to sin,
4. prayer in accordance with the intentions of the Holy Father, and
5. performing the act to which the indulgence is attached.

27. Ferreiros

Spain never ceases to amaze me. I wonder who the no-overtaking sign is for here. Three years later, it's no longer there, and apparently in 2018, it found its rightful place up on the expressway.

The fatigue is slowly accumulating. You start dreaming about how you'll take care of your feet extensively when you get home, how you'll show them gratitude for all their effort. You're already counting the days until you reach your destination. You want to keep walking and arrive as soon as possible. On the other hand, home feels distant and abstract right now. It feels like you've been walking for eternity, and there's no time or space outside the Camino. On one hand, you're on vacation here, away from everyday life, yet at the same time reduced to the simplest, most mundane tasks: finding a place to sleep, washing, eating, possibly tending to wounds. And then walking again.

Today's route seems to be measured in Spanish kilometers again. Besides the cows, something else here reminds me of my childhood on my grandma's farm. The smell of silage – surprisingly not so different from the aroma of the organic cider I drank after O Cebreiro.

I'm used to everyone mistaking me for a German when I speak English. My high school English teacher already told me that. But now, I'm addressed in German before I even say anything. Like today, when I entered the albergue in Barbadelo. Such things happen.

In Silesia we have a joke about the longest bridge in the world – being built along a river. Today on the Camino, I actually came across one.

Walking, as mundane as it is, occupies most of my time and attention. Yet, there's nothing monotonous or boring about it. The daily routine looks almost the same every day, yet I can't find two days that are alike. Not just in terms of new scenery. It's also different thoughts and feelings every day. Even a different muscle hurts each day, a different spot on the foot, and a different strap from the backpack annoys with its squeaking.

Supposedly, people walk the Camino to rearrange their lives and process problems. Then I'm probably doing something wrong because I simply enjoy being here. Perhaps I'm overlooking something, and that's why life outside feels so distant? Or maybe it's about not getting annoyed anymore by the flies that see me as their runway. This thought is slowly becoming abstract and philosophical.

I don't get worked up about flies anymore, but I still do about cow patties. Why don't the Spaniards do it like the Hindus? They would get free fertilizer and heating material, and the poor pilgrim wouldn't have to keep looking down at his feet but could instead enjoy the surroundings.

By the way, I notice that there are actually people along the way who call my German-Spanish pilgrim jargon „Sunday pilgrim." They have backpacks the size of the ones I used for university, white running shoes, a pilgrim staff from the last souvenir shop, and the girls even wear frilly blouses. I can't even remember what color my hiking boots originally were; now they're dirty yellow.

Around noon, I arrive at the albergue. There are hardly any people here yet. Shortly afterward, the woman who spoke to me in German in Barbadelo arrives, with her husband. They're from North Rhine-Westphalia and have been walking the path in stages for 6 years. This time, all the way to Santiago. Finally, a hostel with a kitchen again, and I can eat some of my backpack provisions.

When I return to the dormitory, this time I'm approached by two girls speaking Polish. Now I really have to ask what gave me away in this regard. My walking sticks. As Scandinavian as the company name Fjord Nansen sounds, it's actually a Polish company. The girls also have towels from the same brand. I spend tonight with Jola and Dorota. We treat ourselves to a pilgrim menu and a bottle of wine at the bar a few steps from the hostel. However, I can't fully enjoy the meal because even though I'm now wearing my hiking sandals, the blister under my big toe is throbbing like crazy. And behold, it turns out that Jola is a pediatrician. On the terrace of the albergue, she lovingly tends to my foot. I pierced the blister yesterday in Sarria, but apparently only superficially, while in reality, it consisted of several layers. Fortunately, Jola not only has special blister plasters but also sterile injection needles and expertly operates on my sole. Dorota sits beside us, enjoying the evening sun and commenting on Jola's work with quotes from her favorite series „Grey's Anatomy."

28. Portomarin

In the morning, I'm still undecided about how far I'll go today. Either just to Portomarin, or I'll only attend Mass there and continue walking. It will become clear along the way again. Yesterday, it was definitely the right decision not to go further. Without Jola's help, I would have been in real trouble with the infected blister. In the morning, I gave the girls two of my dehydrated meals and a blister throat lozenge. Dr. Jola was exactly missing this medication in her travel pharmacy, and she has been hoarse since yesterday. That's how it is on the Camino. Somehow, you always meet the people you need at the right time. For me, last night was my little Camino miracle.

The divine providence in our lives is not always so clearly felt, of course. Often, it seems to be the opposite because sometimes everything goes wrong, and it's not our fault. I haven't had to endure any major blows of fate in my life so far, so I can talk for sure. But I can imagine that there are situations where it's very difficult to believe in providence, or even in God's existence. However, when we consider the goal to which providence leads us, some things become at least somewhat clearer. It's not primarily about leading a comfortable and stress-free life here on earth, but above all about attaining eternal life. From this perspective, some of what happens in our lives only makes sense.

Tonight I'm staying at a large modern albergue right at the entrance of Portomarin. It consists of a huge dormitory with probably 200 beds, divided into smaller sections only by curtains. It could be quite amusing at night. Nevertheless, it's still one of my favorite albergues. It has a large dining hall with a modern kitchen, snack vending machines, a beer-tap, and tables outside.

I've just spread out my things on the bed and am about to text Jola to ask if I should remove the blister plaster. The blister underneath seems to have reappeared. In that moment, I receive a message from her: „We're waiting outside the church in Portomarin for the noon Mass. Can you make it?" Once again, she has saved me. I thought there was only an evening Mass and was planning to check later. I hurry to the church and am relieved, because there's no evening Mass today. Jola then attends to my foot again in front of the church. It supposedly looks good. That means the blister will come off along with the plaster. Now, my foot is just loosely wrapped with a bandage, and I'll put on another blister plaster tomorrow. Hopefully, the monster is defeated now. I don't feel like chasing after the girls; they have a much stricter schedule ahead of them than I do. They're continuing on today as well.

But clearly, my guardian angel is watching over my path and even sends me the right people twice if necessary. On the way to the albergue, I stop by a pharmacy. Two Spanish pilgrims are buying something just ahead of me, and with my meager Spanish skills, I understand that they're purchasing a cream for inflamed blisters. I just need to hint that I'd like the same thing they got, along with blister plasters. I wouldn't have been able to explain the anti-inflammatory cream myself. Such Camino miracles are by no means coincidences.

Today's „Menu Peregrino" consists of fish soup, chicken breast, and fruit salad for dessert. By the way, I've gotten into the habit of ordering red wine with fish even if I'm asked. This time, it's even nicely chilled. Well, I dip the ladle into the soup pot and hear a metallic sound. Has a spoon sunk in there? No, it's shellfish shells. Apparently, the fish soup is actually a seafood soup. The rest of the courses hold no surprises.

29.   Portomarin in the morning

I'm standing in front of the post office, waiting for it to open. Apparently, there's a time warp in Spain because not only do the kilometers pass differently, but so do the hours, compared to back home. Last night, I had a little crisis. I need to come up with something for it. If the Camino is sort of a test lab for life, then one can learn methods here that should also work at home. What did I write just the day before yesterday? That I'm just enjoying myself here and not solving any problems? Well, now I don't need to feel guilty anymore. Work catches up with you eventually, one way or another. I give up.

I've given the post office a quarter of an hour past the advertised opening time, apparently they don't want to earn anything from me.

30.   Ligonde

Seven and a half kilometers without a rest area are already exhausting. On the other hand, today's kilometers seem to pass by even faster. I hardly notice the blister anymore. So, it will become clear again during the course of the day where I'll set up my night's lodging tonight.

Unlike Anna, I can't attend today's patronage celebration in Santiago yet, but I watch part of the broadcast on TV in a bar along the way. I also didn't follow Anna's recommendation to stay in Ventas de Naron; instead, I continue on to Ligonde, following the advertising done by both my pilgrim guide and an online forum for the former school. My mood has improved without any particular effort, probably just from the physical activity.

When I see pilgrims with micro backpacks, I can't help but think of the Gospel story about the workers in the vineyard. Even those who only worked the last hour received the same wages. The tricky part is when you walk 700 km on the Camino but fall ill during the last 100 and have to skip a section; then there's no certificate. And now, as I sit on my bed in the small albergue and only hear the arriving pilgrims' phone calls instead of seeing them... Somehow, the purpose of pilgrimage dissipates. You voluntarily give up what you could have learned here. It's like stepping into the shower wearing a raincoat. Learning to trust in providence is part of pilgrimage – that's the difference from a hiking vacation. Someone else might say that pilgrimage is being destroyed by vending machines, cell phones, beer, the internet, etc., and they might be right... Perhaps it's up to each individual what they need to detach from and what they need to learn.

Another invention on these final stages is the „Mochilla-Taxis." Okay, if you're really in dire straits, but apparently the service is used very often. And it reminds me of prayer wheels from Asia. It's probably only a matter of time before someone creates a virtual pilgrim – especially since you can already light a virtual candle in Lourdes. You could send one on the journey, track his blisters on the screen as they change when you add or remove things from his backpack. And the virtual pilgrim would pray for the owner, like the prayer wheel, and send the

Compostela by email. Well, this invention already existed in the past. Many a person who received a pilgrimage as penance and could afford it sent his servant instead... Like in the joke – James, I'm angry, please slam the door.

Sin dolor no hay gloria :)

I've fallen for the „tarta" in the dessert name several times, always finding ice cream hidden behind it, so today I defiantly order „tarta helada" – ice cream cake ;) ... By the way, the Spaniards do have good white wine...

Dad told me on the phone today, following my blog, what I write reminds him of an old song.

> *„ Walking, always walking towards the sun,*
> *until the end of the horizon.*
> *Walking, always walking, without end,*
> *greeting the just awakening day.*
> *Walking, always being on the journey*
> *that people prosaically call ‚life.'*
> *Walking, always walking, as long as possible.*
> *Leaving the coming night behind.*
> *Always walking and safely meeting*
> *the truth's trail blown by the sand."*

On the Camino, you don't actually walk towards the sun until the afternoon, but the lyrics aren't meant to be taken geographically.

> *„Being oneself, undivided,*
> *seeing the world through a child's eyes."*

31. Ponte Campaña

Today, I walk the first nine kilometers again without a break option and also without a stamp. Only in Palas de Rei do I encounter civilization again and find an open post office. I send the wish hat for Jan, some postcards, and a package home with things that I ended up not needing on the way.

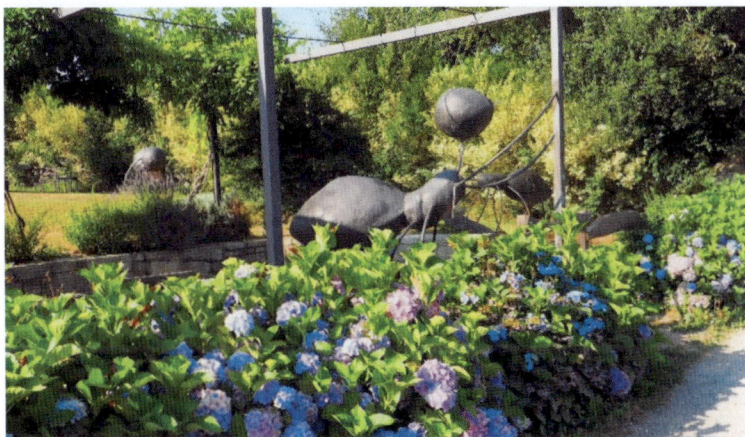

Although it drizzled a bit in the morning, it has now turned into proper summer weather. So, I enjoy a short break in the cool church and treat myself to an empanada for lunch before continuing on. My backpack has become lighter. I still have 69 km to Santiago, and almost five days for it. So, I can afford relaxed short stages. On the other hand, I've become so accustomed to walking that I only stop when I come across a nice albergue.

In 2018, I realize, at the latest on this stage: walking the Camino as a trio is a challenge. My husband hates getting up early, and my mother tolerates the sun the worst of the three of us. Therefore, she tends to walk faster as it gets warmer. We joke about it and take photos of her with a no overtaking sign. I try not to drag my husband out of bed too early and shovel a few things from Mom's backpack into mine.

My Spanish is also getting better and better. At least, that's what I tell myself :D Today, I struck up a conversation with a few Spaniards, and when asked how long I've been on the road, I answered with „venti dios." Well, that would be polytheism. But my fellow pilgrims understood that I actually meant „venti dias" – twenty days. Apart from the fact that „venti" is Italian, not Spanish.

In Ponte Campaña, I come across an albergue in a charming country house. However, the hospitalera says she actually has nothing available anymore. She can only offer me a room without a window, and I should see if I'll take it. I go in and am delighted. Although only a little daylight comes through the door, it's otherwise a dream. Stone walls, a wide couch as a bed, and a faux window with a mountain landscape. A single room for 10 euros. Of course, I eagerly accept, and shortly afterward, I rest my fatigue and the heat of the day on the cool fresh bedsheet. Later, I explore the area a bit and see that this is already the third house at this location. More precisely, always shifted a bit. The previous two burned down, and the next one was built right next to it each time. The sight makes me a little uneasy, and I particularly recommend the night to my guardian angel.

For an additional 10 euros, you can have a communal dinner here. At the long table, there are ten of us, representing 6 countries from Spain to Italy, Greece, Switzerland, the Czech Republic, and Poland. The food is amazing. A 5-course menu: Caldo galega and lentil soup, followed by spaghetti bolognese, chicken with salad, and dessert. Plus, water and bread, as much as you desire. And we manage to finish at least four bottles of red wine in the two hours we sit here.

In 2018, in my cozy single room, there are already two bunk beds, and an opening below the ceiling lets in more light and air. Luckily, I reserved the spots for the three of us in time this time because, as you can also see from the three times as many pilgrims at dinner, this place has become famous.

32. Melide

Yesterday at dinner, I heard about three myths about Spain: first, it's supposed to be flat; second, hot; and third, have good-looking guys. As for flatness, I had no illusions. It's definitely hot since yesterday. And guys? Well, after the two hours that the four fellow pilgrims occupied the bathroom this morning, I expected more extraordinary effects ;) I was about to knock and say, „Girls, hurry up with the makeup," but I don't speak enough Spanish. So, I started relatively late, but still earlier than the guys who overtook me an hour later, singing the Spanish version of the „Maya the Bee" theme song.

A bit later, three pilgrims ride past me on horses. They graze (the horses, of course) a bit further at a bar where I also take a break and devour a delicious hot chocolate pastry with coffee. In 2014, my mother and I also took a break here and met two sisters from Wrocław.

In Furelos – the last village before Melide – there is a picturesque bridge and a church with a special cross, on which Jesus extends his right arm to the people.

In Melide, we find an interesting albergue – in a multi-story residential building. In the covered courtyard, there are washing machines, dryers, and clotheslines. And in the cozy sleeping quarters, there are extra fluffy blue blankets. And as much as I usually dislike using communal blankets, the temptation is too great with this one, and I snuggle up after showering.

Later, we attend Holy Mass and afterwards, we have octopus. There are even special restaurants for it here – Pulperias – and octopus is served on wooden plates with potatoes and semi-dry white wine in bowls.

Four years later, my husband and I decide that after well-spiced octopus, we could crown the evening with something sweet and order iced coffee at another place. The surprise could hardly be greater. We each receive a cup of coffee with milk and a whisky glass with ice cubes.

As it turns out during the night, our cozy albergue has a big flaw – namely, a nightclub nearby.

33. Arzúa

I think my tiredness is slowly accumulating, and as a result, my tolerance level is decreasing. Today, hoping for some cooling down and quiet, I visited two churches along the way because the path is becoming increasingly crowded. Cooling down was indeed there, but quiet – not a chance. In one church, an older lady and her grandson – she didn't look like a grandma, but the little boy addressed her as „Abuela" – were sitting in the front pew and talking on the phone extensively. At some point, she handed the phone to the grandson, who then continued chatting, and then she made the sign of the cross and left. I understand very little Spanish, so it's not impossible that civilization here is simply far ahead of ours, and people are now calling God on their phones.

In the second church, the two ladies who were apparently in charge of the stamp were clearly chatting with each other, loudly. I initially hoped it would be just a brief exchange of information, but after a while, I gave up, left a corresponding note in the guestbook, and moved on. Perhaps I'm becoming a bit touchy?

There are only three days left for me, and that's at my snail's pace. By now, I'm not even tired in the afternoon. In Arzúa, I arrived quite early again. The albergue doesn't open until 1 p.m., so I take a leisurely stroll through the village, do some shopping, and then enjoy the pleasant shade under the plane trees.

In the evening, there is a Holy Mass with a pilgrim blessing in the local church. The church is dedicated to Saint James, it's „little Santiago" for those who couldn't continue. Today, I eat my second-to-last ready meal. It's also my second-to-last night in an albergue. I just received a text from Anna. She's traveled from Santiago to Porto and Fatima with a group of Poles. Why do her messages bother me? Do I feel guilty for going slower than her? Yet, I enjoy every day on the Camino and look forward to the remaining two days.

Somehow, a sad feeling sets in. Something is coming to an end. Three years of dreams, a year of preparation, and now, after a month, it's all over. Supposedly, you become addicted afterward. Today, I met a woman from Austria on the way, who is walking the Camino Frances for the seventh time. I don't think that would be for me. Probably I've simply acquired a taste for hiking again. *(Back in 2011, I didn't think that I would walk the last 100 km twice more, plus virtually the whole CF in 2020, and live in 2023 the first half of it.)*

The pilgrim atmosphere in the albergues is clearly over. Even at half-past ten, people come in making noise, turning on lights, tossing around backpacks and bags, and behaving like they're at Ballermann. Three years later, my mother and I stay a bit away from the center, and it's a much better memory. We cook food in the kitchen and enjoy it on the terrace. The ceiling in the dormitory is high, and the skylights are automatically covered with blinds. And the toilet bowl in the bathroom has shells on the lid.

34. A Campanilla

In June 2014, the weather on this stage is very pleasant. Luckily, it's not raining today, but the sky is overcast, and it's relatively cool. Three years ago, it was one of the warmest days on the journey. Along the way, we meet our acquaintances from Wroclaw again, take photos, and exchange stories. The two sisters are walking to Pedrouzo today, just like I did three years ago. We had planned for a somewhat more leisurely stage, but with the overcast sky, my mother is fully motivated and decides to give it a try as well. Until now, our longest joint stage has been 16 km. At least in Spain; we've done more in Austria, but I'll tell that story another time. If we do manage it today, we'll have time for a short visit to the end of the world before our flight back.

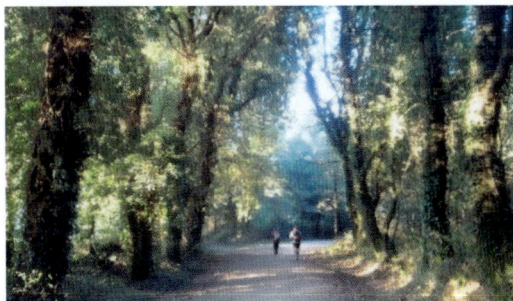

The eucalyptus trees are quite amusing; the bark peels off their trunks in long strips, lying under our feet like the carpets of reeds on Corpus Christi. When the path leads straight to the destination without much risk of getting lost, I let my mother continue slowly and walk the last stretch at a faster pace to secure beds for us in the albergue. Without my backpack, I then walk back to accompany my mother for the final kilometer.

35.   O Pedrouzo

We made it. The large albergue with two floors and a spacious garden has a small courtyard where a little tree grows and water murmurs softly. It certainly has a lulling effect. At the same time, I can't help but think again of the many esoteric reports from the Camino de Santiago. Yet, there is such a significant difference between Christian and Eastern meditation that despite some similar elements, they are completely opposite. They have fundamentally different goals. Christian meditation is neither a concentration on oneself nor a loss of self; it is an encounter with God, the Person. An encounter at the level of the highest faculties of our soul, through which we are like Him – in reason and will. The goal is not the dissolution of one's own self, nor the cessation of thought. On the contrary, even when Saint Paul writes, „*It is no longer I who live, but Christ who lives in me,*" he does not mean some mysterious dissolution, but rather that in every moment, he submits his free will to the will of Christ in order to do what God expects of him.

So, I ponder, sitting next to the power outlet while my phone charges. In the past, a pilgrim was always searching for fodder for his horse or donkey, today for a free power outlet. The girl from the bed opposite me slowly walks past. Her right foot is bandaged, and she now descends the stairs by holding onto the railing with both hands. Thankfully, probably due to my snail's pace, I've come this far without major injuries. The few blisters are hardly worth mentioning.

Three years ago, I ate at a restaurant here and experienced another little surprise. I asked the waitress what one of the main courses was, which was listed in the pilgrim menu, and she answered me in English, saying it was fish. Perhaps she simply forgot to use the plural. This time, I quickly went shopping while my mother, already showered, took her nap. Later, we enjoyed our own pilgrim menu in the kitchen in the garden, consisting of tuna, olives, a hot cup of tea, tomato, baguette, and cider from a champagne bottle. The 20 kilometers deserve to be celebrated.

36. Monte do Gozo

Slowly, I finish my café con leche, knowing that I can only check into the room I reserved at Monte do Gozo at one o'clock anyway. I try to wake up while drinking it because I feel like I only slept in fragments today. In this half-asleep state, I forget my walking sticks at the albergue. It worked out fine three times before, but this time I successfully forget them. The door closes automatically, and although I think I hear a vacuum cleaner inside, no one hears my knocking. And those sticks would have been really useful on this stage of the journey.

Fortunately, I don't fall for the first sign saying „Santiago de Compostela." I'm skeptical enough because to my left is the Santiago airport, which alerts me to the fact that I still have a long way to go. The town I'm passing through is called

Lavacolla because pilgrims used to wash themselves here before entering Santiago.

Maybe we should also remember that before visiting a holy place, we should wash our souls above all else. Sins are a bit like the eucalyptus trees planted here in abundance. People hope for some benefit, but in reality, they drain most of the water from the earth, and the essential oils from their leaves prevent anything else from growing around them, favoring devastating forest fires instead.

Monte do Gozo translates to „Mount of Joy." Supposedly, from here, one can see the Cathedral of Santiago. Or could they in the past? I have no idea. In any case, I'm too blind for that. For the next two nights, I have a room at Ciudade de Vacaciones. On my future Caminos, I won't even consider staying 4.5 km away from the city. But for now, I'll take a shower and treat myself to some sleep. In the afternoon, I'll continue walking to Santiago.

37. Santiago de Compostela

In the afternoon, I put on a dress and head down to Santiago. Somehow, I imagined this city to be much smaller. The last 4.5 km seem to be the longest.

Actually, I hadn't even thought about arriving here. I was so focused on the journey. And now, it surprises and overwhelms me. I turn the corner and suddenly I'm standing in front of the façade of the Cathedral, and suddenly tears fill my eyes.

I AM HERE...

It's a strange feeling, knowing that I don't have to walk anymore, that I've reached my destination. Yes, I can now understand why many here couldn't really stop, but kept on running until they couldn't go any further, because there was only water ahead.

I go inside. First, you have to queue up to reach the large figure of the Apostle in the main altar. They say you should hug him. I have no idea why, but I do it too. In Rome, I even almost climbed over the railing to touch the coffin of my saintly namesake ;)

I continue down to the tomb. Here, I stay a bit longer for a prayer. I have no idea, dear James, whether you actually lie here, or if it's just a beautiful legend. (The tale of the boat made of marble certainly provides enough material for skeptics to mock). In any case, I thank you for helping me make it here.

Later, I line up at the Pilgrim's Office for the Compostela. Whether the plenary indulgence was truly meant for the journey, or perhaps for waiting in line here? The latter requires almost more patience ;)

And I walk back to Monte do Gozo to my room. Along the way, I meet the Austrian woman again, who is walking the

Camino Frances for the seventh time. She likes to talk a lot and tells me that it's freezing cold in Finisterre. As I make my way, I start to feel a bit dizzy, and upon arriving at Ciudade de Vacaciones, I'm relieved to find a comprehensive pilgrim menu in the cafeteria. It's only while eating that I jot down my impressions and upload photos to my blog.

In 2014, my mother and I stayed at the Seminario Menor hostel in Santiago, just one kilometer from the cathedral. Along the way, we also discovered the large market hall and primarily nourished ourselves with fresh fruit for those two days. We bought juicy apricots and our latest discovery, flat peaches, and enjoyed them on the entrance steps of the hostel. While observing the various fishes and seafood at the market stalls, we were only casually interested, sometimes wondering if some of them were sold by the kilo or by the meter. Although the hostel had a kitchen and a large dining hall with a small shop, we were clearly too lazy to cook.

Instead, we discover a pancake restaurant right next to the Cathedral, with delicious „Tarta de Abuela" among the desserts. On one day, we even take advantage of the privilege of a free lunch at the Hospital de los Reyes Catolicos. Originally founded as a pilgrim hostel in the 15th century by the Spanish king, it has now become one of the most expensive hotels in the city. However, for the sake of tradition, ten pilgrims are still provided with free meals three times a day. On this particular day, the influx of hungry pilgrims is relatively small, and we actually manage to be among the ten lucky ones.

It sounds like luck is on our side this year, as we even have the opportunity to witness the famous Botafumeiro swinging twice within three days in Santiago. During the pilgrim Mass, the „Our Father" is recited in Latin. The intention behind this is unity, but unfortunately, everyone ends up praying in their own language. Instead of achieving Pentecostal unity, it becomes more like the Tower of Babel.

38. Finisterre

To Finisterre, I take the bus from Santiago. I arrive at the hotel in the evening and only set out to find the end the next morning. There are still 5 km to the lighthouse, mostly along the coast. Unfortunately, I am accompanied by gray skies and dense fog the whole time. I send a photo of myself with the 0.0 stone back home. Dad replies via SMS: „The old folks in the village say you can see the White House from there." Quite possible, I laugh. Everything in front of me is white right now, so maybe the house too. However, I am compensated for the lack of views later at the beach – I actually find a small scallop shell in the sand.

During my subsequent two visits to the end of the world, the weather is fantastic. I enjoy nature, and my thoughts drift back to the medieval pilgrims. It's funny how many people today believe that people in the Middle Ages thought the Earth was flat. In reality, medieval science was heavily influenced by the realistic philosophy of Aristotle. Saint Thomas Aquinas explicitly speaks of the spherical Earth in his works, citing its shadow on the moon as evidence for him. Even Saint Augustine, who was more inspired by Platonic idealism, considered the Earth to be a sphere, as did other medieval scholars such as Albertus Magnus or Hildegard of Bingen. What the common people believed is likely a different matter, but that's not so different today either. Even today, the general public believes in myths about the so-called Dark Ages, despite evidence from science indicating otherwise.

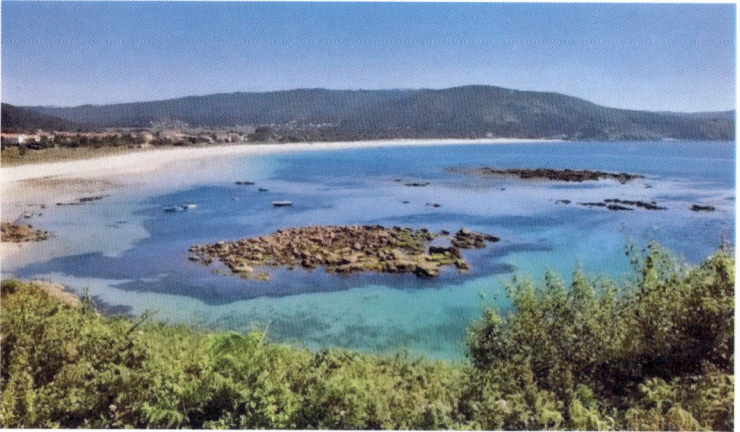

39. Fatima

When planning my first Camino in 2011, it was clear to me –
since I would already be so far southwest, I had to seize the
opportunity and make the additional hop to Fatima. From
childhood, I had a special connection to this Marian apparition
site, despite never having been there. I grew up near the most
famous sanctuary in Poland, dedicated to Our Lady of Fatima.
The main patronage on the first Sunday after May 13 was firm-
ly embedded in my annual program, and we often celebrated
Easter or Christmas there and attended holy masses on other
occasions since my favorite aunt lived in that village.

The bus ride from Lisbon takes an hour and a half. At the
Fatima train station, the next funny surprise awaits – one of
the four languages on the signs is Polish. I leave my heavy
Camino backpack, which now also contains souvenirs from
Santiago, in the hotel room and head to the sanctuary.

At first, all I see is a huge modern concrete building, the
Trinity Church. A bit confused, I walk around, next to the large
crucifix, where Jesus resembles more of a stick insect, and
luckily I then see the old Rosary Basilica in the distance. A sign
directs me to the Adoration Chapel. The entrance resembles
more of a subway station, and the white tiled wall downstairs,
on which someone has drawn Paul's fall from the horse with
a black marker, reminds me more of a public toilet. I enter the
adoration chapel and marvel again – in a sort of wall shelf
hangs a golden square, which I finally identify as a monstrance
with some effort. The 250 seats are practically empty, and
somehow it doesn't surprise me much. I also flee from here

after a short prayer. Upstairs, at the sight of the holm oak and the small chapel marking the site of the apparitions, my heart beats faster. I am here. Some people cross the large round square on their knees, praying the rosary.

To the left of the chapel, I notice smoke. Is someone grilling here? I discover a black marble wall with a long opening where a fire burns. Is this perhaps an artistic representation of the vision of hell that Our Lady showed the children? No, people are throwing candles and other wax items into this opening. It seems to be a kind of offering. Later, in the devotional shop, I discover such figures made of wax: depictions of children or body parts. Somehow unsettling.

I continue to the Rosary Basilica. At least it looks like a church. The interior is quite monotonously dirty white, and I can't decipher the picture in the main altar, but at the graves of the shepherd children, I have tears in my eyes again. A man of order commands me to take off my hat. Now I'm totally confused. Do I look like a man or what? Unfortunately, I can't explain to him that in the Catholic Church, a woman can certainly cover her head and even should; until 1983, it was a requirement based on the Holy Scriptures.

All in all, my Fatima experiences are quite mixed. From the Basilica, I walk to Ajustrel, where the children lived. The path leads through a beautiful Way of the Cross among the olive trees. The three children of Fatima were as much a part of my childhood as the words of Our Lady in Fatima, „Pray the rosary and do penance," which the now-retired pastor always quoted in his sermons. „Sister Lucia Speaks about Fatima" was one of the few books we had at home in German back in the eighties, but I didn't know the language well enough to read it then.

The houses of the children are usually open for visits, but I am too late; everything is already closed. I walk back to Fatima. It is just 2.5 km from Ajustrel to Cova da Iria, where the children used to graze their sheep, but somehow the heat is getting to me today.

In the evening, there is a rosary at the Chapel of Apparitions followed by a candlelight procession on the plaza. I look at the statue of Our Lady being carried and once again have tears in my eyes, hearing the words of the old pastor from Turza between the verses of the same hymn we are singing here: „Mary, you walk among us, you look upon our families, our workplaces, bless us, Mother."

The next day, I am back in Barcelona, at the same hotel where I stayed 33 days ago. This is where the adventure began, and now it ends here. A certain sadness settles in. But does the adventure really end?

40.   a two-item list

Insights from my first Camino:

- Two things I found most useful along the way? A lot of common sense and even more luck. But seriously, a long-sleeved fleece pullover and a good pocket knife with scissors, corkscrew, and such, which could have even pierced my blisters if necessary.

- Two facts about myself that surprised me the most? Firstly, that the hips I worried about the most beforehand never hurt during the journey, and secondly, that I really enjoyed staying in the hostels.

- Two biggest surprises about the trail? Firstly, how often you need that warm pullover, and secondly, the standard in the hostels. Nowhere near like the corrugated iron refuges in the SAT1 documentary.

- Two days with the most beautiful views? The ascent to O'Cebreiro and the sunflower fields in the Meseta.

- Two worst stages? From Terradillos to Sahagún in rain, mud, and cold, and from Virgen del Camino to Hospital de Orbigo, due to sinusitis, partially overgrown trails, and 28 km.

- Two most important encounters? Susan on the way to Triacastela and Jola in Ferreiros, who, through her surgical intervention on my infected blister, probably saved my last week on the Camino. Without her, I would probably have gone to the doctor in Portomarin at the latest, but this way everything was easier. I clearly see divine providence in it.

- Two things I would have done differently? I probably would have walked the first half of the Camino Frances and without room reservations.
- Two things I would have left at home? The survival bag, although one night was indeed so cold that I almost unpacked it. And secondly, my food supplies.
- Two best decisions along the way? Continuing alone and taking a two-day break in Ponferrada.
- Two things I would have taken next time – simply two pullovers.
- Two things that are heavily advertised but I don't need to try again? Caldo gallego and octopus.
- Two things I learned on the Camino? To keep calm until the end in difficult situations and to talk to people even if you don't speak the language.

41.   after the Camino…

The Camino de Santiago has had an unexpected impact on my life. When I embarked on my first Camino in 2011, I wasn't, like many others, in a crisis or at a turning point. On the contrary, I was in the midst of my theology doctoral studies and leading an international Comenius project. However, after the Camino, I slowly began to turn my life upside down. Within a few months, I made the decision to move to Austria. Of the many applications I sent out, I actually received an offer from Tannheim in Tyrol. So, I moved to the Alps. Transitioning to work as a chambermaid just two months before my final examination was unusual, but as they say, every beginning is difficult. It wasn't a long-term solution. The 48-hour workweek of physical labor pushed me to my limits within two months, but it was a start. And in my spare time, I used to explore this beautiful area and take a kind of vacation.

After completing my doctoral studies, I started looking for my next job, this time already residing in Vienna, staying with friends. In early December 2012, I secured a job, at least as a temporary Christmas helper in a bookstore, and just in time for St. Nicholas Day, I also got the keys to my apartment. It was located just 300 meters from a subway station, close to a large market. With a few tricks, I managed to fit all the necessary areas into these 26 square meters, including a guest room. (Once, we even celebrated Christmas there with four people). Shortly after, I returned to the hotel industry, but this time as a receptionist, and I remained faithful to this job for the next few years. That is, until I met my husband and moved again, this time to Germany. The Camino virus, of course, never left me even in Austria and Germany. But that's another story...

42. Hoc(us) est enim…

Since there are many misunderstandings in this area as well, I'll include a small theological addendum here this time. In „Two Cats…", I addressed the topic of indulgences. Perhaps I should explain a little about the Catholic „Hocus Pocus" here. The question of whether, and why not, a non-Catholic should „go to communion" in the pilgrim Mass often arises in Camino groups and forums. The answer is not simply „because we are separate communities." Then the problem would be quickly and easily solved. The issue runs much deeper, and it's not without reason that I link it to O'Cebreiro.

In the widely held conception, now prevalent even among many Catholics, the scene at the Last Supper looked like this:

"While they were eating, Jesus took bread, and when he had given thanks, he broke it and gave it to his disciples, saying, 'Take and eat; this is my body.'" (Matthew 26:26; 1 Corinthians 11:24).

Doesn't something seem missing? Indeed, and that is:

„Τοῦτό μού ἐστιν τὸ σῶμα τὸ ὑπὲρ ὑμῶν κλώμενον"

– *„das ist mein Leib, das für euch hingegeben wird".*

Or in Latin *„Hoc est enim Corpus meum, quod pro vobis tradetur"*, from which the term ‚Hocus Pocus' is derived ;) Not only „that means," not „that symbolizes," not „that is like," but simply ‚ἐστιν' – is. The earliest Christians took these words very seriously.

It's a myth that the belief in the **Real Presence** dates back only to the 16th century. (I discuss the origin of dogmas in the

"Myth-Buster Cat" series on my YouTube channel feles.ama-
bilis). Even though this word doesn't appear in the Bible,
Paul's words essentially convey the same thing in practice:

> *"Whoever, therefore, eats the bread or drinks the cup of the
> Lord in an unworthy manner will be guilty concerning the
> body and blood of the Lord... For anyone who eats and
> drinks without discerning the body eats and drinks judgment
> on himself." (1 Corinthians 11:27, 29)*

For Paul, therefore, the bread during the Eucharist is truly the
body of the Lord. If someone does not discern it from ordinary
bread, it doesn't become any less so. On the contrary – according to Paul, the one who does not discern it is guilty concer-
ning the body of Christ. The claim "if one doesn't believe, it's
just bread for them and nothing happens" clearly contradicts
Sacred Scripture. According to Paul, the bread during the
"breaking of bread" is the Body of Christ, regardless of the
discernment of the recipient. That is the Real Presence.

We also see this deep conviction of the Real Presence in the
writings of the Church Fathers by the reverence with which
every particle of the consecrated bread was treated. The young
Tarzisius allowed himself to be beaten to death by his pagan
companions rather than let the body of Christ be taken from
him and desecrated, as he was taking it to the sick. The early
Christians died for their faith in the Real Presence just as they
died for their faith in Jesus Christ as the only God.

Later, the term ‚**Transubstantiation**' was added. Theology
is a science, and scientists try to express everything as precisely
as possible. Jesus clearly said that the bread is His Body. But
how is this possible when we still see and taste only bread? It
remains a mystery, just as the Most Holy Trinity. However,
attempts were made to explain it a little more closely using
terms provided by ancient philosophy. Essentially, this precise
clarification was only necessary because many false teachings
had spread in this regard. The Orthodox Churches do not need
this term. The belief in the true Body of Christ under the

appearance of bread continues to exist there, as it was the case in the Western Church at least until the 12th century.

The term ‚Transubstantiation' confuses many today because we understand substance completely differently than in philosophy. Therefore, I prefer the German translation ‚Wesensverwandlung' (‚transformation of essence'). Substance, in the philosophical sense, is the essence, what something essentially is. The opposite are accidents. By essence, I am a human being; that is my substance. Whether I have gray hair or pale skin are accidents. Even if I were to lose an arm, I would still be a human being; my essence would not have changed. So what is the substance, the essence of a human being? It's actually hard to grasp. What remains when we strip away all accidents?

In most cases, we deal with changing accidents in life: someone loses their arm in an accident, hair turns gray, bread becomes stale, beer goes flat. That the essence changes while the accidents remain the same happens much less frequently but occurs in some areas of our lives where we have long become accustomed to it. From the moment someone becomes a judge, they can effectively pronounce judgments. Although this is an example of a purely legal transformation, let's go a step higher – to the spiritual level.

A transformation of essence occurs in several sacraments: From the moment we exchange marriage vows, I am a wife. This is not just a symbol, it does not only have a legal significance. My essence has changed with all spiritual consequences, even if nothing has changed scientifically. Marriage is a sacrament (not just the wedding ceremony, but the entire marriage). This means it is an effective sign of God's grace. As a wife, I am in a special way an additional special channel through which God grants His graces to my husband, and vice versa through my husband to me. This transformation occurs at the moment of marriage. Just before that, I was not a wife.

But even baptism (in which all Protestants also speak of

a sacrament) is not just a symbolic admission to the community, but a transformation – from non-Christian to Christian, as Paul even says: new creation, child of God.

Now the transformation of the bread into the body of Christ occurs invisibly and imperceptibly in every Holy Mass. The accidents remain the same. We speak of a Eucharistic miracle (in the narrower sense), however, when the accidents also change simultaneously and instead of bread, the body is visibly present, scientifically verifiable. This happened back then at O'Cebreiro, but it also happens again and again in our days.

About the autor

Pia Lamm – a programmer and PhD theologian, has been walking the Camino de Santiago in various European countries for years and shares her experiences on her YouTube channel feles.amabilis. Her second book, „Two Cats on the Camino," is a continuation of „One Cat..." In it, on her latest Camino in 2023, she delves deeper into her feline nature.

Printed in Poland
by Amazon Fulfillment
Poland Sp. z o.o., Wrocław